Search

A Research Guide
for Writers

Editors
Susan Tierney
Pamela Glass Kelly
Brett Warren

Copy Editor
Cheryl de la Guéronnière

Production
Joanna Horvath

Research
Marni McNiff

The Institute, Inc.
93 Long Ridge Road, West Redding, CT 06896-0811
The Writer's Bookstore
1-800-443-6078
www.WritersBookstore.com

Printed and bound in Canada

CONTRIBUTING WRITERS

Elaine Marie Alphin's articles, stories, and activities have appeared in *HorsePlay, Single Parent, Writers' Journal,* and *The Sondheim Review* for adults, and in *Cricket, Highlights,* and other magazines for children. Her books include the award-winning *The Ghost Cadet* and *A Bear for Miguel* for children. Her novel, *Counterfeit Son,* was the winner of the Edgar Award for Best Young Adult Mystery.

Joan Broerman is the author of a travel book, *Weekend Getaways in Alabama,* and has had articles, stories, and reviews published in *The Louisville Times, The Birmingham News, The Courier Journal, Child Times, A Closer Look, The Writer, Children's Magazine Market,* and *Children's Writer.*

Mark Haverstock is the author of more than 450 magazine articles on a wide variety of subjects. He has written for *Boys' Life, Guideposts for Teens, Guideposts for Kids, Cobblestone, Highlights for Children, Hopscotch, Parenting Teens,* numerous regional parenting magazines, and is a regular contributor to *Children's Writer* and *Children's Writer Guide.*

Suzanne Lieurance's books include *Kidding Around Kansas City; School Projects for Pennies;* and *The Space Shuttle Challenger Disaster in American History,* selected as a Children's Literature Choice. Two more resource books, *The Prohibition Era in American History* and *The Triangle Shirtwaist Factory Fire,* are forthcoming.

Mary Northrup is a reference librarian and a writer. Her credits include *Short on Time, Long on Learning* and *American Computer Pioneers.* She has also published articles in *Calliope, Cobblestone, Turtle, Book Links, Home Education Magazine, Kansas City Star, Writer's Connection, The Family, The Family Digest, Cappers,* and other magazines for children and adults.

Ruth Sachs has written several books about the Holocaust including *Adolf Eichmann: Engineer of Death.* Other titles are *History of the White Rose: The Unfinished Story* and a short story collection, *Something I Heard While Listening.*

CONTENTS

On Your Way   v

Steps on the Research Road   1
by Joan Broerman

Beyond the Basics of Research   9
by Mary Northrup

How to Locate and Use Primary Sources   13
by Mary Northrup

Researching Place: Location, Location, Location   26
by Suzanne Lieurance

Interviews: An Expert Voice to Bring Nonfiction to Life   34
by Elaine Marie Alphin

Electronic Research Tools: What You Need   45
to Find What You Want
by Mark Haverstock

References: In Print & Online   54
by Mark Haverstock

Libraries Online: Content, Not Catalogues   77
by Mary Northrup

Writer Websites: Practical & Fun   85
by Mark Haverstock

Researching People: The Power of Our Family Stories   95
by Ruth Sachs

Online Research: In Search of Photos on the Web   104
by Mark Haverstock

Index   111

ON YOUR WAY

"Find the details that give the past a pulse." "Walk the territory where your subject lived." "Read newspapers from an individual's lifetime." "Get in touch with an expert—someone who is *living* your topic." These are suggestions from writers whose articles appear in this guide—six pros whose practical tips will help you launch your own research for articles, stories, and books.

Writing for today's market demands use of accurate facts, whether you're writing fiction or nonfiction. Authentic settings, believable characters, and specific information supported by well-documented research will increase your publication odds. And the benefits of research are many. On a practical level, research leads to solid content and strong writing. It also opens doors to new avenues of thought, sparking ideas for other projects you'll want to pursue in the future.

This book is not a how-to manual. Nor is it an exhaustive survey of every aspect of research. Rather, *Searching* is meant to give you a sense of what's involved in each basic type of research and to open your eyes to the wealth of resources available to you through libraries, archives, museums, interviews, commercial and government sources, and the Internet. You'll learn where to look for the in-depth research you need, how to move beyond encyclopedias and textbooks, what to do if you have too much or too little information, how to find experts on the Web, and much more. Please note that because Internet sites change frequently, a search engine, such as Google, should be used to help you find a site's updated location.

What's the best way for you to use the information in these pages? Begin at the beginning. Read through all of the articles, and you'll come away with a wide-angle view of research in its many forms. It's a little like traveling to a new place: getting the lay of the land will help you decide which places to visit.

Research will lead you to amazing discoveries—some of them quite unexpected. And research rarely proceeds in a straight line—by its very nature, it's a winding path. So enjoy the process. Research will dramatically improve your writing, and it will also change you. Happy travels.

The Editors

Steps on the Research Road

By Joan Broerman

Who said death and taxes are the only sure things in life? Mark Twain or Will Rogers? To find out takes research. Writers add research to that list of sure things. Whether you write books, magazine stories or articles, fiction or nonfiction, for toddlers, teens, or adults, expect to hear "How do you know?" from a thorough editor, a vigilant librarian or teacher, a sharp-eyed reviewer, or a savvy reader. If you've researched well and documented carefully, you will have an answer.

Editor Karen Grove of Harcourt Brace says the smallest inaccuracy in one writer's work erodes the reader's confidence in both writer and publisher and could impact other writers at a publishing house. "Anything that comes into question reflects on everybody. At Harcourt Brace we want to keep the best interests of all the writers under our umbrella in mind."

Under such pressure to be accurate, how can a writer create? Author Eve Bunting recommends, "Be yourself. That's the only way you can be anyhow. Find the system that works for you." Begin by finding what you care about. Bunting, who has sold 167 books for young people, advises: "Love the subject before you write about it. You won't work up to your potential if you don't."

Step Out

Research begins with identification of a subject that interests you. Your own attic might be a good place to start. Letters, diaries, and journals are primary material prized by historians and biographers. Read voraciously to find ideas. Natalie Bober, a biographer, urges writers to read the sources and find a focus. "Find something you can relate to your own passion." She quotes one of her subjects, Robert Frost: "No tears in the writer, no tears in the reader." Or take a notebook on vacation. Bunting visits historical museums whether she intends to write about the particular area or not. Who knows what ideas will find her?

The critical link of research and true interest exists for writers of both fiction and nonfiction. "You have to have passion or your work will be as dry as a history book. What will stoke the fire?" asks Han Nolan.

How One Writer Keeps Track

For sorting and stacking, writers use a variety of containers, from color-coordinated tubs and labeled boxes to filing cabinets filled with color-coded folders. Index cards of all sizes are popular, but three-by-five-inch cards fit a standard shoe box. Some writers use databases or other computer resources. Whatever the method, a writer must be able to return to references and back up facts.

Tracy Barrett uses three-by-five cards in white and colors. For example, when she wrote her book on Nat Turner, she had heading cards on "Background," "Who Is Nat Turner?" and "Conditions in Virginia." All the heading cards were the same color (pink) and eventually denoted the beginnings of chapters. Her subheadings were blue. She wrote facts on white cards (one fact per card!) and filed the white data cards behind her pink heading and blue subheading cards. As the file grew, she could see whether her chapters were about the same length. She also identified subheadings within her larger subheadings. ("The outline almost wrote itself.") For her bibliography, Barrett keyed her cards to a list of sources. She numbered the first Source #1 and put that number on her data card along with the page number in the source. On a separate sheet, she listed information about Source #1: title, author, library, even the section of the library. She alphabetized her bibliography later.

Snares to Beware

■ Invented Dialogue

Natalie Bober, author of *Abigail Adams, Witness to a Revolution,* winner of the 1995 Golden Kite Award for nonfiction, says the biographer must not invent dialogue. The words of her subjects come from primary material: letters, diaries, journals, manuscripts, and (living subjects') direct quotes.

■ Words Before Their Time

The fiction writer must also watch what characters say. Were the words a character speaks used during the time she lived? Could a Civil War era character invite friends to a picnic? Cheryl Zach, author of a young adult romance series set during the 1860s, depends on a recent edition of *Webster's Collegiate Dictionary* to be sure. The *Oxford English Dictionary* is another source for the history and origin of words and is found in most public libraries. Figurative speech must also be matched with the right time period.

■ Hearing Voices

William Noble, noted writer and lecturer and contributor to *The Portable Writers' Conference* (Quill Driver Books, Fresno, CA), says, "We search for dialogue that will add drama, that will build excitement while staying glued to the facts." Look for dialogue that builds your scene, produces tension, makes a point, and defines your characters. If the dialogue of your experts fails to add to your article, short story, or book, leave it out.

Nolan's young adult novel, *Dancing on the Edge,* received the National Book Award; her *Send Me Down a Miracle* was nominated the preceding year.

Writer Sandra Markle considers herself an information detective who loves science. In following leads on the latest scientific discoveries, she finds and welcomes new topics as a fresh chance to do detective work.

Nonfiction educational publishers offer series that provide a framework in which a writer may be inspired to expand or create. What series have piqued your interest? What ideas does an existing line of books bring to mind?

Reference books for adults and children can also be of use

before you're actually looking up details and facts. Use listings of annotated references to spark thoughts, find information, and brainstorm.

Paths Taken

Once inspired about their subjects, writers take different research paths, but often tread in the same general direction.

Tracy Barrett, who has written about events as well as people, looks first for a general book on the period or topic she has selected, to help her set up a framework. What are the important events, facts, qualities? Next, she makes a rough outline of how to approach her subject, but even as she skims and roughs out, Barrett looks for first-person anecdotes to add important dimension and detail.

"Skim, outline, concentrate," says Jo Kittinger, a science writer. Her routine is to read until an outline takes shape in her mind. Then she takes the broad reading she has done and begins to concentrate her research.

Bober begins by reading several fine, scholarly biographies to get a sense of other writers' impressions of her subject and a jump start on places to look for more sources. She browses in old bookstores and follows a trail from one book to another. Seeking to show how a person's accomplishments were an outgrowth of the life the subject lived, Bober reads newspapers from that individual's lifetime. What was he seeing every day? What was happening in the society around her? "Find the details that give the past a pulse," she advises.

After Bober has read widely, she "walks the territory." For her biography of Thomas Jefferson, she went to Monticello and Paris. Bunting does the same. "Nothing beats being there and absorbing the sensory details. Even if a century has passed, you still get a sense of the place, part of the character's particular corner of the world," she says.

How does a writer prepare to visit and research a setting? Often, a day or two is all time or money will allow. "Keep your objective in mind: atmosphere, time period, or a special event in history," says Cheryl Zach, writer of mystery and historical fiction series. Tour books and works by other authors give her ideas for places she plans to visit on behalf of her characters. When she arrives, Zach looks for local interest books that often cannot be found anyplace else. Writers can fill shopping bags with this kind of material!

When Zach returns from a trip, she sorts her notes, photocopies, and anything else that might be helpful into files such as animal life, geography, or local customs. "Don't skip this step," Zach says. "Common knowledge isn't always accurate. If you mention a particular bird in your story, be sure the bird lives in that setting!"

Zach's research spurs her imagination, giving her ideas for future plots. Kittinger, who recently completed a series on rocks and minerals, expands her research beyond the original subject and works on several projects at the same time.

Markle says that during the research process, information builds. "It will feed into another book, article, or short story." Because information is expensive in terms of time, she determines at least three other uses for it in magazines, newspapers, or conference workshops and talks.

Stops on the Way

That information-building can get out of hand unless writers develop organizing skills, however. Barrett offers this tip to all researchers: "Keep track scrupulously, on cards or computer, of where your references come from, including the actual library branch. It's Murphy's Law. The very fact you need to recheck will be in a library book, and you'll run to the wrong library!"

Such organization eases the way for other reasons, too. Sometimes, Barrett says, the research trail can go cold. A return to the reference will help the writer see the larger context. In Nolan's work on a book about the Holocaust, her notes felt dry. She read her sources a second time to recapture what she felt the first time through.

When help is needed, good record-keeping helps librarians help you. Barrett, like many writers, believes librarians are probably writers' best resources. "They love a challenge!" They also appreciate specifics. The writer armed with names, dates, and places will be prepared to seek help efficiently.

Archivists, like librarians, can best help the writer who has already done some digging. Peter Wilkerson, Senior Archivist at the South Carolina Historical Society, cautions, "There is a fine line between doing your homework—knowing what you are looking for—and thinking you have all the answers."

What is your topic and what specifically do you want to know about it? Write to the archivist and make your question the subject of your first paragraph. What have you already explored? Attach a list. Ask about fees and whether you must make an appointment with the archivist or reserve work space.

Ten Tips for a Trip to the Archives

1. You can bring only pencils and paper into the reading room. Purses, bags, and briefcases are not allowed for security reasons. They may be stored in lockers.
2. Laptop computers with charged batteries may be used. Outlets for computer adapters may be limited.
3. The reference staff is there to help, but must help other researchers, too. The staff will orient you to policies and procedures designed to provide accessibility and protect archival material.
4. Browsing the stacks is usually not allowed in a special library.
5. Be prepared to explain to the reference staff how you know what you already know and what you want to know. (Note: a letter with this information can be sent ahead of time; include time and date of proposed visit. Enclose an SASE for reply.)
6. Plan to take notes. Don't plan on photocopying entire collections. It may take weeks to process a photocopy order.
7. Take careful notes about where you find documents or images (call numbers, containers, files). This will be important to you and the archivist in a variety of ways.
8. Fill out any forms requested by the staff. These aid in planning for the future.
9. Learn how to use the catalogue and find aids to request material more efficiently.
10. Letters of appreciation for good help are always appropriate and appreciated. (With thanks to Peter L. Wilkerson, Senior Archivist, South Carolina Historical Society.)

Both librarians and archivists appreciate thank-you notes from the writers they have helped. Archivists may ask the writer to complete a form to help them plan for the future. These letters and forms indicate the impact of a research facility and can be useful at funding time.

Wilkerson recommends a preliminary meeting between the archivist and writer. During a question-and-answer interview, the archivist listens and thinks, "Which collection? What research strategy?" Every institution has a different set of collections, and an archivist's special knowledge can lead to a writer's exciting discovery.

In addition to librarians and archivists, Kittinger recommends, "Talk with professionals, professors, and hobbyists. Go to museums and clubs. Do field research yourself if the subject allows." Interviews with contacts such as these can be the heart of a piece of writing, and they, too, demand good record-keeping.

Markle, who has more than forty nonfiction books plus a new interactive CD-ROM series about cyberspace aliens to her credit, enlists help throughout her research process. She nurtures a worldwide community of experts in many fields.

Because information in a science book could be four years old before it appears in print, Markle goes where breakthroughs are made. She reads professional journals, searches the Internet, notes credentials, and builds a community of contacts. "Who can you refer me to?" Markle asks. She taps the genius behind the discovery and shares her involvement in what is happening on the cutting edge with her young readers. Markle knows that oversimplification can cause mistakes, so she depends on expert readers to keep her work on target.

Destinations

When is it time to stop research-ing and get down to the business of writing? "You never feel finished with research," says Nolan. "As soon as you have a story or picture in your head and the fire is in you to write, begin!" She does much of her writing and research at the same time, letting each feed the other. "I like the interplay of the two. The work stays fresh and exciting because I'm getting to the point I want to be, which is the writing."

"When writing for magazines, I always read everything I can find on a topic. I photocopy or print sources as I go, keeping my highlighting pen handy to circle the important areas," says Eva Shaw, author of more than 1,000 articles. "In my experience, whether writing for the adult or children's market, editors want the same thing: precision with facts."

Then there is the eternal question, with its own demands on research: "What does an editor want?" Patra Sevastiades, Editorial Director of The Rosen Publishing Group, a nonfiction house that does series for teens and kindergarten to fourth-grade readers, says, "We love writers and want new ideas all the time." But Sevastiades demands precision. Writers must be certain facts are rock solid.

Bonnie Szumski, Editorial

Director of Lucent Books, which publishes for schools and libraries, sees nonfiction as an area of opportunity because publishers are pressured for more books and must look for more writers. Szumski expects writers to fact-check their research and writing and advises them to take two steps before writing a query letter: look at the publisher's catalogue and at the publisher's books. "It's endearing if you can reveal you know something about the publisher in your query letter."

As a fiction editor, Grove admittedly reads a manuscript searching first for a good story, and then for strong characters. The importance of research is third, but it is still important to "make it real. Bring the period to life," she says. Grove doesn't question accuracy unless something jumps out. Anachronisms can jar the reader out of the writer's time period. If, after the initial editing process, an editor feels comfortable with the manuscript, it goes to the copy editor to check facts. A question could be a flag to the editor to go back to the author.

Magazines are excellent markets—and a source of clips—for writers who can research well and write in a reader-friendly voice that connects. And writing articles truly *can* lead to writing books, as Carolyn Yoder, now Senior Editor, History, at *Highlights for Children,* attests.

At children's and adult nonfiction magazines today, documentation is expected and guidelines are explicit. *Muse,* from the publishers of *Cricket, Smithsonian, Living Fit, First for Women,* and many other magazines, request a bibliography listing all resource material, including names, addresses, and telephone numbers of key people interviewed for an article. A growing number of publications also require that "authors should always go to primary sources" before submitting a story.

Love your subject, read widely, find your focus, outline, choose your style of keeping track, ask for expert help, and free yourself to write when the sparks fly. Both Mark Twain and Will Rogers may have said, "In this world nothing is certain but death and taxes," but they were quoting Benjamin Franklin from a letter he wrote to M. Leroy in 1789 (Bartlett, John, 1901, *Familiar Quotations*). ∎

Beyond the Basics of Research

By Mary Northrup

S o you're a writer—and a library user. You know your way around the stacks. You've figured out the features of the online card catalogue. You can use indexes of magazine articles, and you know how to find the facts in general encyclopedias, dictionaries, almanacs, and atlases. Now it's time to go beyond these first steps to do the in-depth research you need for a book, short story, or article.

To do effective research, you need specialized reference tools. The library is full of these sources. Some you may use just once; others will become old favorites as you return to them again and again.

Locate the Specialized

To find specialized sources:

■ Look up your subject in the library's card or online catalogue. Add the subheadings "Bibliography," "Encyclopedias," "Dictionaries," "Directories," "Guidebooks," or "Indexes" to your subject, as in "Clocks—Encyclopedias."

■ Use the *Subject Guide to Books in Print* to find specific titles, whether comprehensive or narrowly focused, on your subject. Look for these in the catalogue, and also browse the shelves in the area where books on your subject are kept.

■ Look for bibliographies in any books you use. They will lead you to more sources and, if you see the same books cited repeatedly in bibliographies or footnotes, you'll know which ones are important.

Sample Search: The Work Astronauts Do on the Space Shuttle

■ If you're writing an article, check the *Reader's Guide to Periodical Literature* to see if this subject has been done. If so, determine the approach and age level and adjust your goals appropriately.

■ Search the library's online or card catalogue for books. Use the subjects "Astronauts," "Astronauts—United States," "Manned space flight," "Space rescue operations," "Astronautics," "United States. National Aeronautics and Space Administration," "Space shuttles."

■ Find more subject headings. To do this, begin with the useful books you've found. The cards or online records for each will indicate subject headings they've been listed under in the system. Also check the Cataloguing-in-Publication (CIP) data on the copyright page (the reverse of the title page) of these books.

■ Use the bibliographies at the ends of useful books to find more possible sources.

■ Check the *Subject Guide to Books in Print* (if you're writing for children, see the *Guide to Children's Books in Print*) and *Forthcoming Books* for current sources.

■ Search *InfoTrac* (http://infotrack.thomsonlearning.com), *Reader's Guide*, and *Applied Science and Technology Index* for periodical articles. Use subjects such as "Space Shuttles," "Space Shuttle Missions," "Astronauts."

■ Search newspaper indexes such as *NewsBank* (www.newsbank.com).

■ Consult the *Encyclopedia of Associations* (http://library.dialog.com/bluesheets) for organizations to contact for information. Look in the "Engineering, Technological, and Natural and Social Sciences" section under "Aerospace."

■ Look for the address or phone number of NASA in the *U.S. Government Manual* (www.access.gpo.gov/nara/nara001.html) and contact them for information, a publications list, and answers to specific questions.

■ Check out a guidebook such as *Find It Fast* by Robert I. Berkman (HarperCollins, 2000), which lists hundreds of sources.

■ If you have a free hour or two, spend it browsing the reference section of your local public library. Start in the subject area of your topic, but also check the bibliography section (Dewey number 016) for guides to information on a variety of subjects.

You'll find many useful reference titles as you become acquainted with your library's collection. Look, too, for any special collections that are shelved separately, such as government documents. (Don't forget to ask for help from the reference librarians. These trained professionals can help you define your search and guide you to the sources you need.) As you become familiar with the wide variety of reference volumes, you'll notice that some of them give you the answer: a biographical sketch, a definition, a statistic, a quotation, a formula. Others are sources to other resources that contain the answer. For example, the *Education Index* leads you to periodical articles. The *Encyclopedia of Associations* provides addresses and phone numbers of organizations that may, when you contact them, give you the facts you need. *Statistics Sources* lists titles of publications that contain statistical information and their issuing agencies.

Everything you need may or may not be at your local library. If you live in a large metropolitan area, investigate other public libraries. College and university libraries are great sources of specialized research tools, and while you probably will not be able to check out materials unless you're a student, you can use the reference area and read and take notes there.

Special libraries run by corporations, hospitals, newspapers, museums, and other organizations are also good sources of information. Check the *American Library Directory* (R. R. Bowker) or the *Directory of Special Libraries and Information Centers* (Gale Research) or call the Special Libraries Association (202-234-4700) for more information on these sources. Access to special libraries varies. Before approaching one, make sure you have defined your research needs well, and call first to see if there are restrictions on use.

Overcoming Roadblocks

No shortage of information or places to get it exists, but some problems may occur from time to time:

■ *Too much or too little information.* Try redefining your search. If you're researching castle architecture in the 1300s, looking up "Middle Ages" will bring you mountains of material. Try something narrower: focus just on French or English castles, even those in a particular area of those countries, or those associated with particular families. If you're searching for information on wooden tops, you may have to expand your search to books and articles on toys.

■ *Confusing subject headings or key words.* You may find yourself at the catalogue saying, "Why can't I find my topic?" Think of all the possible terms and spellings you could use. Look in *Library of Congress Subject Headings* or ask the librarian. For example, you won't find much under "Civil War"—you must use "United States—History—Civil War, 1861–1865."

■ *Access.* It can be frustrating to find a book listed at your library, only to discover it's missing, overdue, or lost. That's the "public" in public library: they can use, and misuse, the books. Try another library or request the book through interlibrary loan. Hate the wait? Plan ahead, and remember: it's a small price to pay for access to millions of books from hundreds of library systems.

■ *Over-researching.* Once you overcome any small problems, you'll discover the joys of research. In fact, some writers enjoy it so much that they just keep going and going and going. Yes, there is such a thing as over-researching. Only you know when it's time to say "Stop!" and get on with the writing.

In research, organization is important. Knowing where you're headed, keeping on track, asking the right questions, taking good notes and keeping them in order, following all promising leads: these practices will make your research projects productive and enjoyable.

Whether you're researching the past for your historical novel or reading about the future for a nonfiction article, get the facts—and much more—at your library.

Sample Search

The sample search in the sidebar on page 10 illustrates one way of approaching a research task. How much information you need and the depth of that information will determine how many research steps are necessary. ■

How to Locate and Use Primary Sources

By Mary Northrup

The best way to write about a person or historical event is by getting as close to the original as possible. Editors suggest, and often demand, that you do not limit your research to encyclopedias. Secondary sources (for example, encyclopedias, biographical dictionaries, textbooks) provide needed information, but original sources give more accurate, personal information, unfiltered through the words of another person.

Original sources can take the form of personal papers (diaries, letters, manuscripts), speeches, interviews, and autobiographies. Travel to historic sites can turn up a wealth of physical evidence to examine. Original records, patents, and old maps can be tracked down to verify facts. Writing about a director? See his or her films. An artist? Examine paintings and sculptures. Historical figure? Dig up old photos. All of these are original, or primary, sources.

Researching original sources is the first step for the writer of biographies. But historical novels, nonfiction articles and books, and historical dramas also cry out for original resources. Even children's picture books can be candidates for this type of research. For her book *Shaker Boy*, author Mary Lyn Ray researched primary sources at a museum and historical village, according to the author notes on the inside back cover.

A search for original sources will take your best Sherlock

Holmes qualities. While many materials are readily available with easy searches at your public library, others require much more digging. Some excellent guides are available to begin your search. Other books will lead you to the materials you need. Still others contain the actual material. The books below are a small sampling of what's available.

So dig in and start the search. The person or event you're researching will come alive as you explore the papers they produced, the items they used, and the history they made. Get to the source!

GENERAL INFORMATION

If you're a beginner at exploring original sources, take a look at these books. You'll find basic information and references to other titles to check.

Knowing Where to Look: The Ultimate Guide to Research

Lois Horowitz. Cincinnati, OH: Writer's Digest Books, 1984. See chapter 18: "Getting It Firsthand: Looking for Original Material."

The Fiction Writer's Research Handbook

Mona McCormick. New York: New American Library, 1988. See chapters on "Diaries, Memoirs, and Biographical Tools" and "Manuscripts, Archives, and Spe-cial Collections."

Ancestry's Red Book: American State, County & Town Sources

Revised edition. Alice Eichholz, ed. Salt Lake City: Ancestry, 1992. A how-to book for finding records of all types, periodicals, newspapers, and manuscripts, arranged by state. Includes list of libraries, archives, and societies.

Genealogical and Local History Books in Print

Fourth edition. Springfield, VA: Genealogical Books in Print, 1985, with supplement to up-date. Local histories can be good sources of information written by participants or witnesses. Look up by state or country.

The Historian's Handbook

Helen J. Poulton. Norman: University of Oklahoma, 1972. See chapter 9: "Primary Sources and Dissertations."

Guide to Sources in American Journalism History

Lucy Shelton Caswell, ed./compiler. New York: Greenwood, 1989. An example of a guidebook for one particular subject. Lists organizations and archives that hold journalists' papers. Includes sections on oral history and data-bases for research.

GUIDES AND DIRECTORIES

Most original materials are found in archives, libraries, and museums. Historical societies and other organizations are also prime places to contact. With the following books, you can find any place, anywhere in the world, that specializes in your research topic. For more, and more specialized, directories, consult *Subject Guide to Books in Print*.

Subject Collections
Seventh edition. Lee Ash and William G. Miller. New Providence, NJ: R. R. Bowker, 1993. Two volumes. First stop for many researchers. Entries are by subject, so you can look for the correspondence of Douglas Fairbanks, Jr., Victor Hugo's manuscripts, or 1880s descriptions of ranch life in Oklahoma—and the library, museum, or university that holds them.

Directory of Archives and Manuscript Repositories in the United States
Second edition. National Historical Publications and Records Commission. Phoenix: Oryx, 1988. Lists institutions by state, then city; provides access information, materials, holdings, and description.

Official Museum Directory
American Association of Museums. New Providence, NJ: R. R. Bowker, annual. 7,500 museums with contact information, collections, hours, publications, research fields, facilities, activities.

Includes related museum, arts, and humanities organizations.

Museums of the World
Fifth edition. Munich: K. G. Saur, 1995. 24,000 museums listed by country, then city. Includes a subject index, which is valuable for the researcher.

World of Learning
London: Europa, annual. This book lists societies, libraries and archives, research institutes, museums, universities, and colleges, along with brief but useful information such as address, telephone, purpose, holdings, and publications.

Directory of Special Libraries and Information Centers
Detroit: Gale Research, biennial with supplements. Special libraries are attached to corporations, law firms, newspapers, hospitals, etc.; specialized collections within larger libraries; and stand-alone research libraries. The five volumes of this book contain more than 20,800 of these libraries, covering a variety of subject fields.

American Library Directory
New Providence, NJ: R. R. Bowker, annual. Lists all types of libraries. Contact information includes name, founding date, population served, circulation, income, and, for researchers, subject interests, special collections, and number of holdings.

Directory of Historical Organizations in the United States and Canada
Fourteenth edition. Mary Bray Wheeler, ed. Nashville: American Association for State and Local History, 1990. Lists 13,000 museums, historical societies, archives, history departments, research centers, and historic sites by state; includes state history offices and index.

Encyclopedia of Associations
Detroit: Gale Research, annual. Newest edition lists 23,000 organizations devoted to any topic imaginable: National Grain Trade Council, American Institute of Graphic Arts, International Banana Association, *Star Trek:* The Official Fan Club.

American History Sourcebook
Joel Makower, ed. New York: Prentice Hall, 1988. More than 3,000 archives, universities, museums, libraries, associations, historical landmarks, parks, and cultural centers are listed, where you can find artifacts, photos, records, maps, manuscripts, rare books, and family and business papers.

Women's History Sources: A Guide to Archives and Manuscript Collections in the United States
Andrea Hinding, ed. New York: R. R. Bowker, 1979. Volume 1: collections by state, then city, with description. Volume 2: index.

Archives of American Art: A Directory of Resources
Garnett McCoy. New York: R. R. Bowker, 1972. Lists artists, dealers, critics, collectors, curators, and a brief description of their letters, journals, photos, and sketches in collections.

ARCHIVE CATALOGUES
Some archives have their own catalogues, which can be found in the reference section of your public library. For example:

The Immigration History Research Center: A Guide to Collections
Suzanna Moody and Joel Wurl, eds./compilers. New York: Greenwood, 1991. Arranged by nationality, with descriptions and lists of newspapers and serials at this center, which is located at the University of Minnesota.

GOVERNMENT SOURCES
Two government agencies are especially helpful in the area of primary sources. The Library of Congress has many divisions for the writer-researcher, including the Rare Book & Special Collections Division and the Manuscript Division. The Library's general address and phone number: 10 1st St. S.E., Washington, DC 20540 (202-707-5000). See the *U.S. Government Manual* for contact information for all divi-

sions. You may also access LC's catalogue through the Internet. Use www.loc.gov to get to LC WEB or Telnet to locis.loc.gov. (Contact LC for their publication "Internet Resources for the Public" for more information.)

The Library of Congress: A Guide to Genealogical and Historical Research

James C. Neagles. Salt Lake City: Ancestry, 1990. Explains the Library's operation, buildings, history, cataloguing, facilities (various reading rooms), collections of interest to historians and genealogists (records, directories, maps, newspapers, periodicals, more). Second half of book lists state sources the Library holds.

Special Collections in the Library of Congress: A Selective Guide

Annette Melville, compiler. Washington, DC: Library of Congress, 1980. Describes theme-related collections housed as separate units in the Library; for example, broadcast recordings of the American Forces Radio and Television Service, Congressional Speech Collection, and personal libraries/papers/manuscripts of a variety of people.

The National Archives and Records Administration is responsible for historical federal documents, presidential libraries, and regional centers. It is located at 7th St. and Pennsylvania Ave. N.W., Washington, DC 20408 (202-501-5502).

The Archives: A Guide to the National Archives Field Branches

Loretto Dennis Szucs and Sandra Hargreaves Luebking. Salt Lake City: Ancestry, 1988. Describes National Archives and Records Administration and each of the eleven branches spread throughout the country. Describes microfilm and print collections at each branch, arranged by federal commission, bureau, and office.

Ask if your library has access to RLIN (Research Libraries Information Network). This electronic database holds millions of records on material held by archives and libraries. (University and special libraries are most likely to have it.)

DIARIES

Of the many types of source materials, diaries can be the most valuable. Since they reflect the diarist's personal thoughts, these may be as close as you can get to a person who is not available for an interview. Women's diaries, especially, are being published, excerpted, and recognized for the pictures they provide of women's lives—the famous as well as the ordinary.

To find diaries in the library catalogue, try the subject "American diaries" (or any other nationality) or the subheading "Diaries" after your subject's name. For events, use the subheading "Personal narratives," as in "World War, 1939–1945—Personal narratives."

American Diaries: An Annotated Bibliography of Published American Diaries and Journals
Laura Arksey. Detroit: Gale Research, 1983. Two-volume set covers diaries written from 1492–1980 by year with brief descriptions. Includes name, subject, and geographical indexes.

American Diaries in Manuscript, 1580–1954: A Descriptive Bibliography
William Matthews. Athens: University of Georgia, 1974. These mostly unpublished diaries are entered under more than 5,000 names. Includes time span, description, and place where located (historical society, library, college, etc.).

And So To Bed: A Bibliography of Diaries Published in English
Patricia Pate Havlice. Metuchen, NJ: Scarecrow, 1987. Arranged chronologically from 838 A.D., with most in the 1800s and 1900s. Provides dates on author, where published, and review, if one exists.

New England Diaries 1602–1800
Harriette Merrifield Forbes, compiler. Topsfield, MA: Perkins, 1923. Citations for diaries and sea journals (published and unpublished) provide name, city, parents, birth/marriage/death dates, diary description, and owner of manuscript (university, historical society, private owner).

The Published Diaries and Letters of American Women: An Annotated Bibliography
Joyce D. Goodfriend. Boston, MA: G. K. Hall, 1987. Annotations include birth and death dates, description, publication location, and complete citation.

Women's Diaries, Journals and Letters: An Annotated Bibliography
Cheryl Cline. New York: Garland, 1989. 2,990 entries, mostly English but some foreign-language; gives citation to where published (book or magazine). Indexes by profession, subject, location, and title.

LETTERS

Like diaries, letters are a very personal form of communication through which the researcher can uncover everyday life, relationships, thoughts, and opinions. You can find collections of one person's letters, such as Emily Dickinson's, George Bernard Shaw's, or Groucho Marx's. At the library, try your subject's name with "Correspondence" as a subheading.

Collections also exist on more specific topics; for example, "American history" or "letters to mothers." Some are general collections, as the following titles illustrate.

The Oxford Book of Letters
Frank Kermode and Anita Kermode, eds. Oxford: Oxford University Press, 1995. Read the letters of Sir Walter Raleigh, Abigail Adams, Charles Dickens, Elizabeth Barrett Browning, John Steinbeck, and many more in this anthology that covers the 1530s to 1980s.

Famous Letters: Messages and Thoughts That Shaped Our World
Frank McLynn, ed. Pleasantville, NY: Reader's Digest, 1993. Here are letters that made a difference or make history more complete; by Vincent Van Gogh, Mary Shelley, Napoleon, Joan of Arc, and so on.

MANUSCRIPTS
Manuscripts can contain diaries, letters, and other personal papers. Often unpublished, these items can also be uncatalogued or even unorganized. At your library, look up "Manuscripts—[state or country or language]" for guides to collections. The Library of Congress has a whole division dedicated to the collection of these items. Contact the Manuscript Division, 101 Independence Ave. S.E., Washington, DC 20540 (202-707-5383).

National Union Catalog of Manuscript Collections
Washington, DC: Library of Congress, 1959–, annual. Contains information on approximately 50,000 collections held by 1,300 institutions; personal, business, government, church, and society papers.

Index to Personal Names in the National Union Catalog of Manuscript Collections 1959–1984
Alexandria, VA: Chadwyck-Healey, 1988. Two-volume set is a research tool for above title; lists name, dates (sometimes), and manuscript number.

A Guide to Manuscripts in the Presidential Libraries
Dennis A. Burton, James B. Rhoads, and Raymond W. Smock, compilers. College Park, MD: Research Materials Corp., 1985. Covers materials available at the libraries of Hoover, Franklin D. Roosevelt, Truman, Eisenhower, Kennedy, Johnson, Ford, Reagan. Includes brief descriptions and availability to researcher.

Civil War Manuscripts: A Guide to Collections in the Manuscript Division of the Library of Congress

John R. Sellers, compiler. Washington, DC: Library of Congress, 1986. Describes materials (papers, diaries, letters, letterbooks, and so on), who person is, state, years covered, how many items.

Members of Congress: A Checklist of Their Papers in the Manuscript Division, Library of Congress

John J. McDonough, compiler. Washington, DC: Library of Congress, 1980. 894 Senators, Representatives, and Continental Congress Delegates listed, with short biographical information and type of materials with dates.

AUTOBIOGRAPHIES

Often biographies and autobiographies are grouped together; for example, on the library shelves and in some indexes. Biographies are great sources of information, but autobiographies are primary sources for the researcher, since they contain the subject's actual words. (Use biographies to examine their bibliographies; some may contain citations to primary sources.)

A word of caution: authors can "forget" certain parts of their lives or embellish on what really happened. As with all research, try to verify in at least two sources before accepting anything as fact. The first six titles below are bibliographies that guide you to writings; the remaining are examples of volumes that contain actual autobiographical selections.

American Autobiography 1945–1980: A Bibliography

Mary Louise Briscoe, ed. Madison: University of Wisconsin, 1982. More than 5,000 citations to autobiographies by the author's name; provides birth/death dates, bibliographic information, annotation.

A Bibliography of American Autobiographies

Louis Kaplan, compiler. Madison: University of Wisconsin, 1961. Companion to above title. Covers works published before 1945 only.

Through a Woman's I: An Annotated Bibliography of American Women's Autobiographical Writings, 1946–1976

Patricia K. Addis. Metuchen, NJ: Scarecrow, 1983. Wide variety of standard autobiographies, journals, collections of letters, travel narratives arranged by author with dates. Indexed by profession, subject, and title.

Black Americans in Autobiography

Russell C. Brignano. Durham, NC: Duke University, 1984.

More than 700 names; mainly post-1865 titles. Includes annotations and several indexes.

Jewish Autobiographies and Biographies
David S. Zubatsky. New York: Garland, 1989. Look up by name; citation includes dates, brief description of person, list of auto- and/or biographies. Covers 1st century A.D. to present.

British Autobiographies: An Annotated Bibliography of British Autobiographies Published or Written Before 1951
William Matthews, compiler. Hamden, CT: Archon, 1968. Arranged by name, with indexes by professions, places, wars; for example, governesses, inventors, sports journalists, Napoleonic War, country house life, exploration in India.

Contemporary Authors Autobiography Series
Detroit: Gale Research, 1984–. Authors write about themselves, with bibliographies of their work. Includes photos.

Bearing Witness: Selections from African-American Autobiography in the Twentieth Century
Henry Louis Gates, Jr., ed. New York: Pantheon, 1991. Covers 1904–1990; Richard Wright, Langston Hughes, Maya Angelou, Alice Walker, more.

When I Was a Child
Edward Wagenknecht, ed. New York: E. P. Dutton, 1946. Excerpts from autobiographies, concentrating on childhood. 41 selections, including Jane Addams, A.A. Milne, Mark Twain.

SPEECHES

We move now to much more public forums. It is possible, in speeches and lectures, to hear the author's own "voice": his or her opinions, views, experiences. The first entries below index speeches, either generally or those of a particular group.

Speech Index
Fourth edition. Roberta Briggs Sutton. New York: Scarecrow, 1966. *Supplement 1966–1980* by Charity Mitchell (1982). Look up by subject or speaker (or use title index); entry refers to book in which the speech appears.

Index to American Women Speakers 1828–1978
Beverley Manning. Metuchen, NJ: Scarecrow, 1980.

We Shall Be Heard: An Index to Speeches By American Women, 1978 to 1985
Beverley Manning. Metuchen, NJ: Scarecrow, 1988. Companion volumes arranged by author (speaker) with citation to book, periodical, government document, or proceedings that con-

tain the speech. With subject and title indexes.

The following volumes give the actual text of speeches.

Vital Speeches of the Day
Mount Pleasant, SC: City News Publishing, semi-monthly. A staple in most public and school libraries. Indexed in *Reader's Guide;* with annual index (November) mailed to subscribers; also cumulative indexes.

Representative American Speeches
New York: H. W. Wilson, 1937/38–, annual. Includes speaker index in each volume; also 10-year indexes.

Voices of Multicultural America
Deborah Gillan Straub, ed. Detroit: Gale Research, 1996. 230 speeches by 130 African, Asian, Hispanic, and Native Americans from 1790 to 1995. With photos; ethnicity and subject indexes.

Lectures in America
Gertrude Stein. Boston: Beacon, 1985. Reprint of 1935 volume. Example of book of speeches by one author. For subjects who were or are public speakers, it's worth looking here for collections of their speeches.

INTERVIEWS
Perhaps the best way to get to know a person about whom you are writing is to talk to him or her. A skilled interviewer can elicit much from a willing subject. If that person is still alive, perhaps you can arrange an interview; if not, or if a personal meeting is impossible, their interviews may show up in some of the following sources. Newspapers and magazines also carry interviews; use a periodical index such as *InfoTrac* to find them.

Interviews and Conversations with 20th-Century Authors Writing in English: An Index
Stan A. Vrana. Metuchen, NJ: Scarecrow, 1982. 3,500 interviews with 1,600 writers, poets, and playwrights are indexed by the subject's name. Citations to magazine articles and books.

The NPR Interviews 1995
Robert Siegel, ed. Boston: Houghton Mifflin, 1995. Consists of text of actual interviews, about 2 to 4 pages each. (This book is not indexed.)

The Get Ready Sheet
Utica, NY: Mid-York Library System, biweekly. Lists upcoming national television and radio interviews for authors and their books, including show and date.

ORAL HISTORY
Oral histories take the interview form further; they attempt to capture an era or a subject by recording the words of the peo-

ple who lived through it. Very often these people are the ones who would otherwise have had no place in written history. At your library, look for indexes, as represented by the first three titles below or for the actual oral histories (several examples follow). For more information, contact the Oral History Association, P.O. Box 97234, Waco, TX 76798-7234 (817-755-2764).

Studs Terkel is also well-known as an oral historian. For examples of his work, see *Hard Times: An Oral History of The Great Depression* (New York: Pantheon, 1970), *"The Good War": An Oral History of World War II* (New York: Pantheon, 1984), and others.

Oral History Index
Westport, CT: Meckler, 1990. Lists 30,000 oral history transcripts held in 400 oral history centers in the United States, Canada, Great Britain, and Israel.

Oral History in the United States: A Directory
Gary L. Shumway, compiler. New York: Oral History Association, 1971. Lists schools, libraries, historical societies, institutes, foundations by state; describes major topics, purpose, number of interviews, hours of tape, pages.

Guide to Kentucky Oral History Collections
Cary C. Wilkins, ed./compiler.

Frankfort, KY: Kentucky Oral History Commission, 1991. Example of regional focus. Thousands of oral history interviews arranged by repository (museum, library, etc.); states how many interviews, how many hours, time period, access, brief description.

Baseball Chronicles: An Oral History of Baseball Through the Decades
Mike Blake. Cincinnati: Betterway, 1994.

These Are Our Lives: Federal Writers' Project of the Works Progress Administration
Chapel Hill: University of North Carolina, 1939. Life in the Depression-era South.

You Must Remember This: An Oral History of Manhattan from the 1890s to World War II
Jeff Kisselhoff. San Diego: Harcourt Brace Jovanovich, 1989.

NEWSPAPERS
First-hand accounts of historical events often appeared in newspapers. The sources below can help you track down papers and articles. If your topic is of local interest, try your library's or historical society's collection of hometown papers.

Gale Directory of Publications and Broadcast Media
Detroit: Gale Research, 1990–, annual. Formerly *Ayer Directory of*

Publications from 1869. Arranged by state, then city; lists newspaper's founding date, frequency, contact information.

Poole's Index to Periodical Literature, 1802–1906
William Frederick Poole. Boston: Houghton Mifflin, 1882–1908. Two volumes, plus supplements. This is the standard reference for historical research in this type of literature.

History and Bibliography of American Newspapers, 1690–1820
Clarence S. Brigham. Worcester, MA: American Antiquarian Society, 1947. Provides a publishing history of each title, plus where it is held: library, historical society, university. Arranged by state, with title index.

Native American Periodicals and Newspapers 1828–1982
James P. Danky, ed. Westport, CT: Greenwood, 1984. Example of specialized subject index. Arranged by title, with many indexes. Provides title, dates of publications, frequency, description, publisher and place, subject focus, and library that holds.

RECORDS
When it comes to records of lives, there is no shortage: there are literally millions of records. Fortunately, many "finding" aids help genealogists who search for family records. As a writer, you can use these guides to find sources that verify facts and establish time lines. Search for vital records (birth and death); marriage and divorce records; census, court, land, tax, immigration, military, prison, school, hospital, and employment records. Where are these records? County clerk offices, federal archives, courts, businesses, associations, genealogy libraries. Find out where to start by consulting a general guide (see "Guides and Directories" above); then move on to specialized indexes.

The Sourcebook of County Court Records
Second edition. Tempe, AZ: BRB Publications, 1995. Lists more than 7,000 courts by state, then county with city cross-references. Provides information on contact, access to records, what can and cannot be released, turnaround time, cost. See also *State Public Records* and other locator books by the same publisher.

U.S. Military Records: A Guide to Federal & State Sources, Colonial America to the Present
James C. Neagles. Salt Lake City: Ancestry, 1994. Presents various resources, including National Archives, military history centers, Library of Congress, Daughters of the American Revolution, Veterans Affairs offices, and

much more. Also includes post-service and civilian sources.

National Directory of Churches, Synagogues, and Other Houses of Worship
Detroit: Gale Research, 1994. Four-volume set, with 350,000 places of worship, by region, state, city, and denomination.

Passenger and Immigration Lists Index
Detroit: Gale Research, 1981, with supplements to 1995. Covers sixteenth to mid-twentieth centuries. Lists name, age, place and year of arrival, accompanying passengers, code to source book (published passenger lists, naturalization records, church records, local histories, voter registrations, and land records).

MAPS

Are you doing historical research? Tracing a pioneer's journey? Trying to establish your subject's residency at a certain time? You may need maps. The range here is broad: from crumbling maps sketched by prospectors to state-of-the-art satellite photo maps. For specialized information, contact the Library of Congress Geography and Map Division (202-707-8530) or the U.S. Geological Survey, 12201 Sunrise Valley Dr., Reston, VA 22092 (703-648-4305).

Guide to U.S. Map Resources
Second edition. David A. Cobb, compiler. Chicago: American Library Association, 1990. Lists museums, libraries, historical societies, universities by state, then city, with specific strengths, special collections, holdings, chronological coverage, availability.

Cartographic Records of The Bureau of Indian Affairs
Laura E. Kelsay, compiler. Washington, DC: National Archives and Records Service, 1977. Lists maps of the various divisions of the Bureau, with description, date if available, and whether published or unpublished.

CONCLUSION

Research into primary sources can be some of the toughest but ultimately most rewarding research you will ever do. Although a valiant effort has been made by bibliographers, librarians, scholars, and archivists to organize many types of materials, many primary sources lie uncatalogued or even undiscovered in attics, file drawers, and other nooks.

But to read the letters, journals, or other words of the person whose biography you are writing, or those of someone who lived through the time you are writing about, is a treasured experience.

Research—and enjoy! ■

Researching Place:

Location, Location, Location

By Suzanne Lieurance

Sure, location is the most important factor for realtors and homeowners. It's also a major concern for writers, yet most don't have the luxury of working on location. Instead, they do the majority of their work at home, using a variety of research techniques to make specific locales come alive for their audiences. Here's how to uncover those special details that let readers know you've been to the places you're writing about—even if you haven't!

Travel Electronically

Lisa Harkrader lives in a small town in Kansas. A couple of months ago, she was writing a novel set in the Australian outback and needed to find out how to throw a nonreturning boomerang. She couldn't just take off for Down Under. Instead, Harkrader traveled the Internet. She located a website for a company in Australia that sells the boomerangs.

"I e-mailed the company, explaining who I was and what I was doing, and asked if they knew where I could find the information I needed," says Harkrader. "They e-mailed back with very detailed instructions on how to throw a nonreturning boomerang. These are the kinds of details that are hard to uncover when you can't actually visit a place, so you have to be creative and relentless in tracking them down."

Julia Beiker also lives in Kansas. When she was writing a story that takes place in Italy, she journeyed through the Internet, too. She joined an Italian genealogy group online to get a feel for how to enhance her story. Beiker says, "An Italian professor gave me expressions that would have been used by a boy during the time period of my story." (See "Researching People, The Power of Our Family Stories," page 95, and an accompanying list of online genealogy sources.)

Now here's a switch. Kristin Nitz lives in Italy and her current novel is set in Tuscany. "I used Yahoo (a search engine) to look at rentals in the Italian countryside," Nitz says. "The house and grounds I created for my setting are a composite of several of those villas."

Kim Williams-Justesen writes travel guides and usually does visit most of the places she includes in her guides. Yet she also goes online for some of her research. "I look at the government sites because it's amazing what you can find there, especially for state and national parks and historic sites," says Williams-Justesen. "I visit travel sites that might have reviews of places that I'm going to review—but I do this after I've visited a particular site, so their review doesn't color my own perception."

When Jane Buchanan, who writes historical fiction for kids, was working on a picture book set in 1910 Dorchester, Massachusetts, about a Polish family's first Thanksgiving celebration, she found, "The hardest part of that story was finding confirmation that factories in the Boston area would have been operating on Thanksgiving day in 1910. For that I used the Internet. I found articles on the library's magazine article index and tracked down their authors on the Web. I also came across a labor history listserv and people there were most helpful."

Study Maps

For writer Nancy Ferrell, the first step in researching location is to "obtain a map, as detailed as I can get, for the city and country I'm writing about. A map lets the writer know how far it is from point A to point B—important information that's often needed to make the action in a story credible."

Wendie Old, a children's librarian for more than 30 years who also writes fiction and nonfiction, agrees. "It helps to have a map. That way you're consistent as you move your characters from place to place."

Maps can be obtained from your local library, but the Internet is also a good place to find all kinds, everything from highway to weather maps.

When you're writing a historical book and "not on the scene," says, Suzanne Hilton, author of more than 20 books, "one aid is a topographical map that shows just the mountains, streams, and such—no highways, etc." She recommends the Library of Congress for "extremely early maps." Contact the Library of Congress about travel brochures, flyers, and pamphlets.

The picture books of Verla Kay take place in a variety of locations. Kay has written about the California Gold Rush, the railroad, covered wagons, and many other elements of U.S. history. "I've written successfully about places I've never been," says Kay, "but it's much easier when I've been there in person." She obtains brochures, flyers, and pamphlets from chambers of commerce, travel agencies, and the local visitors' bureaus for the locations she writes about, as a starting point for her research.

Williams-Justesen also sends away for materials. In one of her children's stories, a young girl goes to Ontario in search of a long lost uncle. To find out about Ontario, she says, "I sent away for brochures and maps and got a lot of really good stuff for free."

In the Neighborhood

With so many reference materials available online today, writers can sometimes forget about the resources at libraries. Besides local public libraries, college and university libraries offer a wealth of materials. Many have extensive archives of national magazines that include articles about locations all over the world. These magazines, old and new, often contain detailed photographs that can be immeasurably helpful for writers who need to see what a city or town looked like years ago or how it appears today.

"I can't emphasize enough the value of a good reference librarian," says Buchanan. "It's amazing, the things librarians can find that the average person simply wouldn't know existed. Never be afraid to ask for help. The librarian who is good won't give up until a source to answer your questions is found. It's amazing what you can find in a library if you know, or have help finding out, where to look!"

Other sources at your fingertips are the videos you can find at your library and video store. They have countless documentary videos that can provide writers with facts and tidbits about areas all over the world. Harkrader found additional information for her novel set in Australia this way. "To learn what aboriginal music sounded like," she says, "and to get a sense of the speech rhythms of aboriginal children from the Northern Territories, I found a nonfiction video in the library."

Most larger cities have their own magazines that can give writers a glimpse of what goes on there. San Diego, Santa Fe, Kansas City, Boston, New York, Atlanta, and many, many other cities publish magazines that contain a variety of articles about local spots writers can include in their fiction, or use as background information for their nonfiction. Many of these magazines have websites where writers can find articles from current and back issues. Other publications, like *Southern Living, Midwest Living,* and *Sunset Magazine* offer articles and advertisements about broader sections of the United States.

Large bookstore chains like Borders and Barnes & Noble carry European magazines that cover topics like fashion, home furnishing, and architecture. These are sometimes helpful for getting a feel for a country the writer hasn't visited.

Travel to the Past

Writers can't actually travel back in time to see what a location was like long ago. Or can they? Never underestimate the power of museums.

When Hilton was researching her book *The Way It Was—1876,* she found a way to see how the World's Fair in Philadelphia would have looked that year. "At the Franklin Institute, there was a perfect scale model of the entire World's Fair of 1876. By scrunching down and looking through the gate, I could see the layout as a person entering the fair would," Hilton explains.

"Museums, libraries, and archives are treasure houses of old newspapers, diaries, and photos," says Jeri Chase Ferris, who writes biographies and historical fiction. "I'd say every one of these was an absolute necessity when researching the locations where my subjects have lived."

Sometimes sources are closer to home, no matter how geographically distant. Elaine Marie Alphin needed background information about El Salvador when she was writing her award-winning book, *A Bear for Miguel.* "My family on my father's side is from El Salvador," says Alphin. "While the war was going on, my grandmother wrote me letters telling me how hard it was on the family, on my cousins. So I was drawing in part from their experiences."

Even if you don't have family letters about a faraway place, when writing about a specific place in an earlier time in history, many writers find it helpful

Places Please

A Few Great Resources for Researching Location

Maps
- **The Weather Channel:** www.weather.com
For weather maps of all areas of the United States.
- **GIS Data Depot:** www.gisdatadepot.com
For free topographical maps of many areas in the country.
- **Library of Congress:** http://catalog.loc.gov
101 Independence Ave. S.E., Washington, D.C. 20540 (202) 707-5000.
A database of approximately 12 million records representing books, serials, computer files, manuscripts, cartographic materials, music, sound recordings, and visual materials in the Library's collections.
- **Savewealth.com:**
www.savewealth.com/links/travel/maps/index.html
For city maps and travel maps for regions all over the United States.

Magazines
- *National Geographic:* http://www.nationalgeographic.com
Available by subscription, but you can see articles from past and current issues at the website.
- *British Heritage:* www.britishheritage.com
The magazine of history, culture, travel, and adventure for those who love England, Scotland, Ireland, and Wales. British Heritage explores Britain's natural beauty, historic sites, famous and everyday people. See sample articles at the website.
- *Historic Traveler:* www.historictraveler.com
6405 Flank Drive, Harrisburg, PA 17112.
The Guide to Great Historic Destinations. Each issue is packed with features and guides to historic places, hotels and inns, reenactments, tours, side trips and more. Complete with beautiful photography and maps.

Government Sites
- **Govspot.com:** www.govspot.com/state/
To locate state home pages, type in the name of the state you want to research.

(continued on next page)

Places Please *(continued)*

Online City Guides
■ **LookSmart:** www.looksmart.com
Searchable data of information about cities in the United States.
■ **ClickCity:** www.clickcity.com
Searchable database with information about cities and states throughout the United States.

Museums
■ **The Franklin Institute Science Museum:** http://sln.fi.edu/
222 North 20th Street, Philadelphia, Pennsylvania 19103.
■ **Smithsonian Museum:** www.si.edu/
For information about the museum write: Smithsonian Information, SI Building, Room 153, Washington, DC 20560-0010.

General Books
■ **Encyclopedia Smithsonian** www.si.edu/resource/faq/start.htm
This online encyclopedia features answers to frequently asked questions about the Smithsonian and links to Smithsonian resources from A to Z.
■ *Fodor's* **Travel Guides** www.crazydogtravel.com
Fodor publishes travel guides for cities and countries all over the world. You can find these guides at local bookstores or at online booksellers.
■ **Lonely Planet Travel Guides and Phrase Books:**
www.lonelyplanet.com
Guides to cities and countries (and various languages) all over the world. These guidebooks are available at Amazon.com or at the Lonely Planet website.
■ **The Handy History Answer Book:** by Rebecca Nelson Ferguson. Available at local bookstores.

Books on Specific Times and Places
■ *The Writer's Guide to Everyday Life in the 1800s,* by Marc Mc-Cutcheon
■ *Everyday Life During the Civil War,* by Michael J. Varhola

(continued on next page)

Places Please *(continued)*

- *The Writer's Guide to Everyday Life in the Wild West (from 1840-1900),* by Candy Moulton
- *The Writer's Guide to Everyday Life in Regency and Victorian England (from 1811-1901),* by Kristine Hughes
- *The Writer's Guide to Everyday Life in Renaissance England (1485-1649),* by Kathy Lynn Emerson
- *The Writer's Guide to Everyday Life in Colonial America (from 1607-1783),* by Dale Taylor
- *The Writer's Guide to Everyday Life from Prohibition Through World War II,* by Marc McCutcheon
- *Everyday Life in the Middle Ages (The British Isles from 500 to 1500),* by Sherrilyn Kenyon

One More Great Source
GORP (Great Outdoor Recreation Pages):
http://www.gorp.com/gorp /location/us/us.htm
Information about every state, as well as national parks and other travel destinations.

to use diaries from that period. Many historical societies have a variety of diaries, according to date. Hilton suggests, "The University of Georgia put out a book called *American Diaries in Manuscript, 1580-1954, A Descriptive Bibliography.* It's an index to diaries *not* published, their dates, and where in the United States they can be found. I'm not sure you can still buy one, but it's a real find."

When Debra McArthur was researching her book about the Dust Bowl, she took an unusual approach for obtaining primary sources. McArthur is a college instructor in the Midwest, so she figured there were people around who had firsthand memories of the Dust Bowl, or knew someone else who did. To find them, McArthur created a flyer describing her project and asking for help. She placed the flyer in the college library and other high traffic areas throughout the campus when the college was having its alumini weekend.

Marty Crisp, author of 11 books, is another writer who likes to visit the location if at all possible. "In the case of my current project, set in England in 1599, I can't of course find 1599, but in England, I came pretty close!" she says. "I went to old manor houses and palaces searching for the perfect setting, and when I found it, it was practically a ruin. It was a manor house built in the 1580s and stripped down to its walls, but it was so much easier to furnish with my imagination than to strip out all the 1700s, 1800s, and 1900s things in other old houses that were in better repair."

Capture the Essence

Old has been lucky enough to live within driving distance of most of the locations where her subjects have lived and worked. "I visit, take pictures, talk to people there, take the tours and listen to the patter of the guides. Just the way things are said can be different, special, catchy," she says.

"Although it's not possible sometimes to visit the sites I write about, I certainly try," says Ferrell, who lives in Alaska. "There's nothing like actually being there and, once there, having some exciting hands-on experiences that help me transfer that excitement to my readers." When Ferrell wrote *The U.S. Coast Guard*, she arranged through the rear admiral to fly in a search-and-rescue helicopter in Sitka, Alaska, where she could take photographs from the aircraft.

For her book *Gratefully Yours*, about a girl who rode an orphan train from New York to Nebraska in 1923, Buchanan thoroughly researched Nebraska, but as the deadline for completing the manuscript neared, she began to feel uneasy. "It would be immediately apparent to anyone who lived in Nebraska that I was a fraud, I was sure. I panicked," she says.

She told her husband she had to go to Nebraska. He politely pointed out why she couldn't go right then, so the book was published without Buchanan ever setting foot in Nebraska. A week after the book came out, an older woman told Buchanan that she had grown up on a farm in Nebraska. "I don't know how you did it," said the woman, "but you have captured it. This is where I grew up."

"I was thrilled, of course, and flattered, and also relieved," says Buchanan. "It was important to me to make the story believable, and also as accurate as possible."

There are all sorts of ways to research location. It doesn't really matter how you conduct your research— just so you convey the reality of place. As Hilton says, "I'm an avid researcher because some 10-year-old kid can tell if I'm guessing, and I don't want that to happen." ■

Interviews:

An Expert Voice to Bring Nonfiction to Life

By Elaine Marie Alphin

Nonfiction research once meant spending time in the library reading encyclopedias and reference books, dipping cautiously into periodicals and professional journals. Then the first writers to navigate the growing Internet discovered access to a vast cyberspace reference "library." As more writers learned to be good researchers, however, so did readers. Many adults (as well as kids) now surf the Web more often than they pick up a magazine or book. If writers use the same sources as those kids and adults, readers probably won't want to read a rewritten simplification. And an editor won't want to publish it.

To give readers more than they can find for themselves,

you need to go beyond what someone else has written. You need to get in touch with someone who's *living* your topic—you need to speak with an expert in the field.

"A lot of authors get notes back from editors that say, 'This is a good topic, but there's no life here' or 'We really don't get to know this person' or 'The piece lacks focus'," says Andy Boyles, Science Editor at *Highlights for Children*. "One way to solve those problems is to talk to an expert."

Writers often shy away from hands-on research. They don't know any experts—where could they possibly find someone to interview? Perhaps they're shy about approaching complete

Experts Online

If you know the expert you're looking for but don't know how to contact him or her, online research can help you find your source.

Contacting a Designated Expert

Research may show that your expert teaches at Pomona College. Go to a listing of American universities at www.clas.ufl.edu/CLAS/american-universities.html and find Pomona College. Click on it, and you'll be transported to its Web page. From there, go to the listing of faculty and staff and search for the expert's name by department. You'll find a phone number and, most often, e-mail and postal addresses. Send the expert an e-mail or a letter requesting an interview.

If your expert is farther away (say, teaching at Oxford University in England), don't worry—the Web stretches wide enough. Many college websites also have links to international universities, or use a major search engine to access this information. If your expert is affiliated with a museum, you could track him or her down by getting a listing of museums at: www.icom.org/vlmp/index.html*museums and clicking on the appropriate museum to jump to its Web page.

Locating an Expert

Sometimes you don't know the name of an expert to contact, and are searching for someone in a particular field. A good way to locate an interview source is to join an electronic newsgroup or mailing list. There's no charge for an electronic subscription; mailings from the group will automatically be deposited in your electronic mailbox. Read the postings for a few weeks, and you'll probably see one or two people who are articulate, explain things well, and look like good candidates. Members of professional mailing lists and newsgroups usually sign their posts with their academic or professional titles, so you have an idea of

(continued on next page)

strangers and asking them to explain their specialties for freelance articles. As struggling writers, they may even feel inadequate in speaking with a successful scientist or artist or athlete. While it's true that some professionals are too busy to give interviews, most enjoy talking about their work and like the idea of

Experts Online *(continued)*

who you are considering, and you can e-mail them requests for interviews. Universities provide students with academic accounts, however, so check the academic faculty listing to be sure that this "professor" exists, and when you carry out the interview, phone the department and ask to be put through to the professor, to be sure that a student or teaching assistant isn't borrowing someone's identity online.

Engineering a Search
In case your research and your online eavesdropping fail to connect you with the right expert, don't give up. Try a search engine. The main ones are listed in the article "Electronic Research: What You Need to Find What You Want" (page 45).

Suppose you're looking for an expert on architecture. You can type in "architecture" to start with and search—but chances are you'll get far too many listings. Narrow your field by using the topics provided. For example, in Yahoo! you might scroll down to "arts and humanities," then choose "architecture." From there you could jump to "architects," and from there choose commercial firms or personal exhibits and click on Web pages with phone, fax, or e-mail connections.

If you draw a complete blank, you can always search for a recommendation. Go to: www.askanexpert.com/ and enter your topic or search by category. This URL provides links to Web pages where you can ask an expert any question—but be sure to do the background research to ensure that your "expert" is really an expert!

Another source is ProfNet at: www.profnet.com/profnet_home/index.html. This search engine allows you to send questions to nearly 4,000 public information officers around the world.

---

having people read about them and their accomplishments.

What an Expert Offers
Fred Bortz, author of five books and more than 40 magazine articles, finds inspiration for nonfiction in the science books he reviews and in scientific talks he hears, and he uses this inspiration to explore these topics for children as well as adult readers. "I see an angle I like, and turn it around to write it," he explains. "Sometimes the theme and angle are right for kids, but the topic

Phone, Online, or in Person?

Once you're ready to do the interview, you have to decide whether to do it from a distance or up close. E-mailing questions and receiving answers can work for distant subjects (given the time difference, it could be awkward to interview someone in China otherwise), but e-mail replies tend to be stilted. Phone interviews work better if you can't travel to meet with your subject. "It's always better to do it in person," advises science writer Fred Bortz. "You see the person in the work environment and can talk to other people associated with your main interview. In a phone interview, you aim for thirty to forty-five minutes, an hour at the most. In person, you start at an hour and go from there."

The real issue, however, is the added expense of a face-to-face interview. "For an article, it's not really justified," Bortz admits. "The questions are much more focused on a single topic—you try to ask questions that get the interviewee to talk a lot. In a magazine interview, I have them talking to me and I reinterpret. In a book interview, those questions are still the heart, but I can set them up with shorter questions to get them thinking more along the lines of what my audience might want—they're talking to the kids themselves. It gives them a chance to size you up, to connect themselves more directly to your readers and not see you as an intermediary."

wasn't aimed at kids originally. I say, 'Hey, I can do that!'"

Hearing an expert speak gives you a good opportunity to introduce yourself and ask if you might get in touch later about an interview. Usually, however, you'll want to find an expert for a topic you've already read about. You can write your article without doing an interview, but chances are you'll get the manuscript back from the editor. If it shows enough promise, the editor may specifically ask you to add an interview.

According to John D. Allen, Associate Editor of *Cricket*, "Sometimes it works out to send things back and ask authors to research more deeply. In that situation, the manuscript is something shy of a complete article. With a little extra direction, an author can find what is needed in a particular spot to flesh out the article."

What writers need is personal

input from someone in the field. According to Boyles, "The things you get from an interview that you can't get from book research are direct quotations, lively anecdotes, firsthand impressions, and some insight into the subject that may not come through in other venues—in other words, an entryway into the article, something that will crystallize your focus."

"This can be much more important in magazine writing than in books," Melissa Stewart, Senior Science Editor at Grolier, points out. "Most books don't have direct quotes unless we're trying to get very current information, as discoveries are being made. In some series, of course, interviews are essential. Our To the Young. . . series consists entirely of interviews with professionals in certain fields, and our social studies series consists of diary entries from historical periods."

Stewart notes that "interviews are important and a good research source, but that doesn't mean that the writer *has* to use direct quotes in the book." It depends on the age you're writing for. "We almost never use direct quotes for kids," Stewart explains. "At the adult level, however, it can be nice to throw in a few quotes to get the flavor of the topic."

Finding the Elusive Expert

The first challenge is finding an expert to interview. "In some cases," says Bortz, "I know enough about the field that I can identify a whole bunch of potential experts. In that case, the hardest part is trying to deduce who's going to be a good interview. If an expert has tried to write for the popular market, it shows a willingness to get away from the stereotypical test tube and talk to people."

If you don't know anyone in the field, a recommendation from a friend can help. For example, Bortz was looking for a scientist to interview about the chemistry of buckminsterfullerene ("buckyballs") and related molecules. He heard from a former colleague that Richard Smalley of Rice University was very forthcoming when he spoke to college undergraduates. "Based on that," explains Bortz, "I knew going in that he would understand enough about my audience to give the right balance between the technical details and the human side."

Writers can also turn to the Internet for help. (See the sidebar on page 35 for ideas to start your search.) Bortz also recommends putting a posting on an Internet bulletin board asking readers "Who would you like to interview?" and "What would you like to ask them?" He explains, "Obviously, if you have friends who are interested in the subject, you ask them—and these days your friends are on the Internet."

But not just any expert will do. "I always have some criteria in mind when I do the search," Bortz says. "It's not just that the science is good and interesting, but also that the subject is human and genuine."

Boyles agrees that it's important to get input on potential interview subjects. "If you want to write about science," he advises, "you need to develop a cadre of friends who are willing to accept a phone call—some confidants who will help you find your way when you're trying to decide whether or not this is a topic to pursue."

There are also book sources, such as *Who's Who,* that can help you locate an expert. *Dial-An-Expert: The National Directory of Quotable Experts* by Marc McCutcheon comes out with a new edition annually. One advantage of this source is that the professionals listed in it have agreed to be included, which means they're willing to be interviewed.

Sometimes your reading will point you toward a specific interview source from the beginning, but he or she doesn't respond, or simply says no. "Sometimes it will just kill an article if you can't reach a person," Bortz admits. "It goes into your file of good ideas that just didn't quite work." Or the person you originally wanted to interview may have another idea. "I really wanted to interview one scientist who courteously said no," Bortz recalls. "But he also said he was no longer active in the field and recommended another scientist. I was disappointed, but the contact he recommended turned out to be exactly right. You just have to be prepared to redirect. You have to know what your goals are so you can understand when redirection will be appropriate."

If you've worked with an editor before and the article is an assignment, the editor may well suggest an interview source. But watch out for sending a proposal to an editor who doesn't know you, and asking for a recommendation for a source. "When you set out to write an article," says Allen, "you should have a strong enough interest and background in the topic to know who you're looking for. If you come and ask me, 'Who should I interview?' it will make me think you really hadn't done much work. But if you send me a strong article that's missing an aspect, I may well suggest an interview and recommend a source if I can. That's different from coming to me in the beginning and asking for a source."

Preparing for the Interview

Once you zero in on your topic and select an expert, it's time to plan how you intend to conduct the interview. This is where techniques diverge: there are as many ways to run a successful interview as there are writers.

Most interviewers believe that it's important to do your homework and become familiar with the topic before you contact any potential interview subject, but not all. "Some writers advocate going in cold, open as a babe," says Boyles. While this can certainly make the interviewer more receptive to the wonder of the subject, Boyles cautions, "It's easy to miss important ideas because you're trying to understand the basics—they're trying to talk about Shakespeare, and you're still on the ABCs."

Instead, Boyles advocates researching the individual you plan to interview as well as the subject matter and terminology in advance. "If you're serious about presenting yourself as a professional, you need to have a good handle on the topic before you go in," he says, and points out that you need to go beyond an encyclopedia introduction. "Ask experts to have someone on their staff give you references to some of their recent papers, and read them."

Writers also have different views on how to contact the source to schedule the interview. Some like to phone the subject as their first contact. This lets you explain in person what you plan to do in this article and why you want to interview them. Particularly if your enthusiasm spills over into your voice, this can make a good impression and sway their decision to give you the interview—many people are susceptible to impulse buys. Bortz warns, however, "On the phone they may say, 'Oh, no, not another interview.'

"I prefer to contact them in writing with some details about the project and give them time to reflect." He points out, "The hard thing is knowing whether or not you've actually reached them, and how long to wait—you must pursue them courteously. When you follow up, you hope to get their secretary because you don't want to interrupt them at work."

It's important to remember that experts are busy people. You have to impress them with your professionalism and let them know that you're willing to work

Take Notes or Tape-Record?

Some writers like to take notes during the interview, while others opt for tape-recording. The advantage to taking notes is that writing the quotes takes longer than the instantaneous recording of a machine. People are uncomfortable with silence, and often the subject will inject comments into the silence that prove wonderfully illuminating.

The disadvantage, of course, is the danger of missing something. That can also be a disadvantage of relying on technology, however. A bad tape or a recorder that's low on batteries can leave you without a record of your interview, so double-check your equipment. Despite the risks, science writer Fred Bortz advises taping. "You can be so focused on getting the words down on paper that you miss the meaning. I can't get all the nuances of the conversation if I take notes, and to me the essence is often in the nuances. So I take the somewhat risky step of relying on technology for the words while I make notes and listen for the nuances. I use two tapes of different lengths so I don't become so entranced in the interview that the tape runs out and I have to ask the person to repeat. There's also the possibility that words can be garbled on tape; the second tape may be clearer."

around their schedule.

If an editor has assigned the article, it's easier for the writer to show the expert that this is worth the investment of time. Most articles, however, are written on spec. "*Muse,* our newest magazine, does commission articles," says Allen, "so they give people the documentation they need to pursue interviews. We don't commission articles at *Cricket,* but occasionally we give a writer a letter of interest to show the interviewee. We have to be careful about this, because we don't want to mislead the author into thinking that it's an acceptance of the piece in advance. If it doesn't get published, things can get ugly."

Not only the author can suffer from an interview-based article that doesn't pan out. Boyles says, "I'm reluctant to give a firm go-ahead to beginning authors. Experts control the interviews they give because they hold their time to be valuable. The same person won't want to grant multiple interviews for the same magazine, so the magazine has something at stake." If the first article doesn't work out and the author said it was a definite piece for a specific magazine, another writer may have trouble interviewing the expert by saying the piece is aimed for the same magazine.

The writer should always be honest with the subject by making it clear whether the piece is an assignment or on spec. That honesty is the first step in establishing a relationship that will lead to a successful interview.

Connecting With the Subject

"You need to earn the subject's trust for this sort of 'one-hour friendship' by recognizing where the subject is coming from," says Boyles. "You're each doing something for each other. You're getting an article; they have to get something too." Often the subject is happy to have a willing listener—this is where your advance research in the field pays off. "A scientist goes to picnics or family reunions and can't talk to people," explains Boyles. "People ask him what he does, and he tries to tell them, and their eyes glaze over. He has maybe three friends in the world who understand what he's saying. If you can make yourself that fourth friend for an hour, you can have a great interview."

Once you've made that connection with your subject, you get him or her talking. Have an idea of the direction you would like to take with the article

before you start, and prepare a written list of questions that will focus your subject on the aspect of the topic that interests you. "One of the most important things you must do to make a connection with your subject," says Bortz, "is to have a well-designed interview protocol when you go in, but know when to deviate based on what they say. Being able to make that decision on the fly is a very important skill."

And it's a good idea to have those questions prepared before you phone or write to make the initial contact to schedule the interview—often you'll catch the subject at just the right moment, and he or she will suggest doing it immediately rather than scheduling it for later.

Sybil S. Steinberg, a writer at *Publishers Weekly* and author of a book on interviewing, says, "Although every assignment represents a different challenge, I have one unwavering rule. At the end of every interview I ask the subject the same question: 'Is there anything you wanted to talk about that I haven't asked?' This almost always produces useful, colorful material."

After the Interview

Upon transcribing your quotes from the interview, you're faced with two concerns. The first is the question of accuracy—just because your expert said something, that doesn't make it true. "I'm a scientist," Bortz says. "You always have to look at your evidence with healthy skepticism. It's not that I don't trust them, but people don't always remember things perfectly. If there's a significant fact, I'll double-check. If anything sends up a red flag, I'll follow it up."

Allen agrees. "If an expert tells you anything that conflicts with what you think you know, check with a third source to make sure you understood the interviewee originally, and also to make sure that the interviewee hasn't made a mistake."

This doesn't mean that a writer must get multiple confirmations for commonly accepted facts. For example, Allen points out, "for most children's articles, people aren't really getting into a contested spot. One interview may be enough, depending on how deeply the topic is explored or whether it's on the cutting edge." Boyles adds, "You're also working with your editor, and the editor should have a sense of whether a new development is going to be upsetting apple carts."

The second concern is how the expert sounds. "People tend to hem and haw," warns Stewart. "They're not always articulate,

and we emphasize proper English in our books." Allen agrees. "You want your authorities to speak grammatically, which people do not. You want your quotes to sound as polished as the rest of the article. If they're not, it makes the expert look like less of an authority."

Boyles adds, "Writers can leave out the ahs and the stammering—that's just making the subject sound good. Who could complain? You get into trouble when you've misunderstood something. A subject may give you the same idea three times, and say the first part clearly once, the end clearly later on, and the middle most clearly the third time. You go through the interview and put the parts together so they read smoothly. That's fine as long as you don't violate the spirit of what they were trying to say, so it's a good idea to call back and read such quotes aloud, or send a fax so they can read their own quotes."

This practice is called "cooking the quotes," and writers must be careful to check any changes with the subject, because misrepresenting what the subject says and putting incorrect ideas into his or her mouth will spoil a good writer–subject relationship and could even leave the writer open to accusations of libel.

Some editors who are used to the newspaper business might disagree with checking the quotes with the source. Unless your interview leads to a dramatic exposé that the interviewee would be unwilling to confirm, however, it's better to get that confirmation. "It's very important to get back to the source to check the quotes," says Allen. "You don't want to leave the interviewee with the feeling that you're out to take advantage. You should want to represent the subject accurately."

After finishing the article, be sure to thank your subject for giving you his or her time. Most writers send a copy of the published piece to their source, or ask their publisher to do so. "I almost always try to follow up," says Bortz, "especially if they've given me an indication they care about seeing it. In fact, I'd be disappointed if they didn't. I guess I'd think I'd found the wrong person." And following through on a successful interview lays the groundwork for you to return to that subject for a related interview in the future, or to ask his or her help in referring you to a good source for an article about a different topic.

Well Worth the Work

Do interviews sound like a lot of effort? Allen would agree. "Inter-views are more work than spending hours reading," he admits, "and it's hard because you have to find the person and break through the ice. Probably for this reason, interviews are the one thing in nonfiction that aren't done enough. Book research is a wonderful thing, but finding an authority to interview is what elevates a common article to an exceptional one."

Exceptional articles sell. The next time you get a quirky nonfiction idea with sure-fire reader appeal, bring it to life by augmenting your book research with an expert interview. In addition to making a friend who'll enhance your enthusiasm for your topic, you'll increase your chances of seeing your work in print. ■

Electronic Research Tools:
What You Need to Find What You Want

By Mark Haverstock

Many writers buy computers solely as word processors, and some dabble in e-mail or computer games. But few ever learn their computers' other talents—it's like having a Ferrari in the garage and only driving it to the market for an occasional load of groceries.

Besides acting as your high-tech typewriter and mailbox, your home computer can also be a high-powered research assistant. Although it won't (and probably shouldn't) eliminate trips to the library, it can cut your research time considerably and provide you with resources you never knew existed.

CD-ROM References

Your computer already has two built-in references (a spell checker and thesaurus), but you'll probably want more. Practically any general reference you have or want in hardcover is available in some electronic form. One advantage of using electronic CD-ROM references is the ability to sift though massive amounts of information quickly, using key words or short phrases you supply. Electronic media are also cheaper than print versions, so having a complete reference library at your fingertips is more affordable than ever. You can compile a basic reference collection for a little more than a hundred dollars, one that takes up less than an inch of shelf space.

The first shelf of your electronic library should include a variety of commonly used references.

Internet Citations

Many editors request lists of sources showing where you obtained your information for a magazine piece or book. It helps their fact checkers and establishes your credibility. With the constant evolution of the Internet, it's even more important to document sources for your own records. "You're not assured the same things will be there in six months," says Ellen Bates, a professional researcher. "The most important thing to do is date the information and download it if it's something you'll want later."

What about bibliographies? *The MLA Handbook for Writers of Research Papers* now contains information about citing online sources. For an authoritative explanation of the full MLA system of documentation, see the *MLA Handbook*.

The following are sample entries for citing Internet sources. These samples can also be found at www.mla.org on the Internet.

Basic form:

Author's Last Name, First Name. "Title of Work." *Title of Complete Work*. Date of electronic publication <Electronic address or URL of source>.

Scholarly project:

Victorian Women Writers Project. Ed. Perry Willet. Apr. 1997. Indiana U. 26 Apr. 1997. <www.indiana.edu/~letrs/vwwp/>.

Professional site:

Portuguese Language Page. U of Chicago. 1 May 1997 <http. humanities.uchicago.edu/romance/port/>.

Book:

Nesbit, E. *Ballads and Lyrics of Socialism*. London, 1908. *Victorian Women Writers Project*. Ed. Perry Willett. Apr. 1997. Indiana U. 26 Apr. 1997 <www.indiana.edu/~letrs/vwwp/nesbit/ballsoc.html>.

Poem:

Nesbit, E. "Marching Song." Ballads and Lyrics of Socialism. London,

Internet Citations *(continued)*

1908. Victorian Women Writers Project. Ed. Perry Willett. Apr. 1997.Indiana U. 26 Apr. 1997 <www.indiana.edu/~letrs/vwwp/nesbit/ ball-soc.html#p9>.

Article in a reference database:
"Fresco." Britannica Online. Vers. 97.1.1. Mar. 1997. *Encyclopedia Britannica.* 29 Mar. 1997 <www.eb.com:180>.

Article in a journal:
Flannagan, Roy. "Reflections on Milton and Ariosto." *Early Modern Literary Studies* 2.3 (1996): 16 pars. 22 Feb. 1997 <http://unixg.ubc.ca:7001/0/e-sources/emls/02-3/flanmilt.html>.

Article in a magazine:
Landsburg, Steven E. "Who Shall Inherit the Earth?" *Slate 1* May 1997. 2 May 1997 <www.slate.com/Economics/97-05-01/ Economics.asp>.

Posting to a discussion list:
Merrian, Joanne. "Spinoff: Monsterpiece Theatre." Online posting. 30 Apr. 1994. Shaksper: The Global Electronic Shakespeare Conference. 27 Aug. 1997 <www.arts.ubc.ca/english/iemls/shak/MONSTERP_ SPINOFF.txt>.

Personal site:
Lancashire, Ian. Home page. 1 May 1997 <www.chass.utoronto. ca:8080/~ian/index.html>.

Microsoft Bookshelf integrates ten different reference works: *Encarta Desk World Atlas, The American Heritage Dictionary, Roget's Thesaurus, The World Almanac, The Concise Columbia Encyclopedia, The Columbia Dictionary of Quotations, The People's Chronology, National Five-Digit ZIP Code and Post Office Directory, Microsoft Computer and Internet Dictionary,* and *Encarta*

Desk Encyclopedia.

Infopedia also squeezes an entire bookshelf of information into CD-ROM format. You get instant access to the 29-volume *Funk and Wagnall's Encyclopedia, Merriam-Webster's Dictionary of Quotations, Merriam-Webster's Dictionary of English Usage, Webster's New Biographical Dictionary, Hammond World Atlas, Roget's 21st Century Thesaurus, The World Almanac,* and *Merriam-Webster's Dictionary.*

Next, consider a CD-ROM encyclopedia set. CD-ROM encyclopedias combine the text of traditional encyclopedias, but they're much easier to use and generally much less expensive. You can search for specific information using key words or phrases, or browse using built-in guided tours, time lines, or topic lists. Most include more pictures than their print counterparts, along with a selection of sounds and video clips. Microsoft's *Encarta Deluxe Edition* is the best-selling multimedia reference, containing more information than a traditional 29-volume encyclopedia. Jump text, a series of 300,000 cross-references, lets you move quickly to related articles. *Encarta* also goes beyond the basic CD-ROM by linking with more than 5,000 websites for additional updated information.

World Book and *Grolier* take similar approaches, linking their articles to current information accessible on the Web. They contain all the text of their print versions, while incorporating multimedia sight and sound. Each includes an atlas, and *World Book* goes one better with a complete dictionary.

If you're looking for in-depth information and can forego the multimedia features, *Britannica CD* is the ultimate CD-ROM encyclopedia for researchers. It contains the complete text to *Encyclopedia Britannica*—all 32 volumes. Though it's a bargain compared to the print version, it's still pricey compared to other electronic encyclopedias.

Internet Reference Sources

You'll find an assortment of references on the Internet, most of which are free. They're good alternatives to purchasing your own copies of resource books—especially those you use infrequently. To reach these sites, type the URL (the Internet address enclosed in parentheses) into your Web browser.

Billed as a one-stop reference desk, **Research-It** (www.itools.com/research-it) provides a combination of quick-search tools in the areas of language, library reference, geography, finance, mailing, and the Internet. Some of the more interesting features include a universal translator that translates a word in any language to a large list of foreign languages; computer, anagram, and acronym dictionaries; and a variety of sources for on-screen maps. This site also contains more conventional references, such as a standard dictionary.

Looking for a phrase, but can't remember where you found it? **Wisdomquest** (www.websonar.com) is a huge library containing everything from the classics to video transcripts. If "To be or not to be?" is the question, enter the phrase. Before you can say *Hamlet,* Act III, you've got the source.

The WWW Virtual Library (www.vlib.org) has the distinction of being the Web's first distributed subject catalogue. Alhough its list of categories is limited, each item provides links to some of the best Web pages available. Some of the notables include African studies and the history of science, technology, and medicine.

Global Internet Searches

The Internet is the largest repository of knowledge on earth. It's grown to the point where it can provide virtually any type or format of information. In addition to text, it offers archives of graphic materials—maps, charts,

illustrations, and photos. There's a lot of good, useful information out there, but finding exactly what you need—efficiently—is the key.

Web search engines commonly bring up too many sites to cope with—sometimes hundreds or even thousands—ranked by someone else's definition of relevance. Looking at each possibility is time-consuming. Frustrated, you try to narrow your search or, in desperation, try another search engine—only to come up with the same result.

One Web page that's a "must read" is **Using the Internet for Research** (www.purefiction.com/pages/res1.htm). This guide was compiled especially for writers and gives no-nonsense tips and answers to frequently asked questions (FAQs) about finding information on the Internet. Be sure to check this page out before cranking up one of the popular search engines on the Internet.

There are dozens of search engines on the Internet, but the following are among those that will routinely deliver relevant hits. You'll find some search tips listed to help you make the most of each one.

AltaVista (www.altavista.com) is still an excellent site to use when you're looking for the obscure topic—the needle in the haystack. It also does well with more common topics if you narrow your search parameters from the start. One way to do this is to put quotation marks around names. *"Grover Cleveland"* produced about 1,000 responses, almost all of the top 20 about the former president. Typing *Grover Cleveland* without quotes produced about 30,000 Web pages containing that word combination, including subjects further from the target, such as *presidential memorabilia* or *Grover Cleveland Williams.*

Excite (www.excite.com) has one of the most complete and up-to-date catalogues on the Web. Using the Sort-by-Site function can improve the relevancy of responses. If you find a particularly useful site, choose "Click here for a list of documents like this one" to find additional related sites.

Infoseek (www.infoseek.com) provides a great variety of sources and uses advanced search techniques similar to those found in AltaVista. It also has a unique image-search function that displays thumbnail images rather than just shuffling you off to a website. Be sure to check out "Related Topics" above the list of search results. This area will usually give you some helpful suggestions for expanding your search.

Yahoo! (www.yahoo.com) is an entirely different animal. Built like an index, it's a directory to the Web that's compiled and classified by a group of people. Yahoo!'s human intervention has it strengths and weaknesses. The half-million listings in Yahoo! are categorized more relevantly than a computer search engine could ever do. But other search engines find websites automatically that Yahoo! may not know about, and the listings will be more up-to-date.

Ask a Researcher
Sometimes a computer search engine isn't the best way to get to specific information. If you're tired of wading through the hundreds of document summaries returned by computerized search engines, **HumanSearch** (www.humansearch.com) serves up information the old-fashioned way —with the human touch.

The first step is to search the HumanSearch database of already answered questions—provided for free. If you can't find what you want, you can submit your own question for a flat fee. When you submit the question, don't use key words—phrase your question as if you were asking a reference librarian for help. From there, your question is sent to a distributor, who assigns it to a qualified searcher. The searcher then retrieves all the information he or she can find, in the form of answers and websites. These answers are read by an inspector to verify that they're relevant, then sent back to you via e-mail. Turnaround time is about 48 hours or less.

Ask Jeeves (www.aj.com) is a fast and easy way to find answers to questions. Ask Jeeves a question in plain English and, after interacting with you to confirm the question, Jeeves takes you to one (and only one) website that answers your question. This free service uses a combination of computer smarts and human research—it consists of thousands of question templates and millions of researched answer links to websites.

The Newsstand

Many newspapers, periodicals, and newswire services now have sites that are easily accessible on the Web. Some, such as *USA Today* (www.usatoday.com), feature current headline news and keep limited back issues. Others keep more extensive searchable archives that date back several years. Though all offer some free text, some may ask you to register on the site and may charge modest fees for premium services or downloading articles. For example, the *Boston Globe* (www. globe.com) charges $1.25 to download an article at off-peak hours (6:00 p.m. to 6:00 a.m.)

One stellar starting point for periodicals is the *American Journalism Review* (AJR) NewsLink (www.newslink.org/ menu.html). AJR has assembled a comprehensive collection of more than 4,000 world-wide links to newspapers, magazines, TV and radio networks, newswires, and news services on the Web. Make your first stop the "Starting Point for Journalists" list.

In conjunction with Yahoo!'s Search Index, **Reuters** (http:// news.yahoo.com) provides hourly news summaries as well as search capabilities through Reuters' extensive news story archives.

The Electronic Newsstand (www.enews.com) is home to 200 magazine sites and has comprehensive links to 2,000 other magazine-related sites. At the least, there are sample articles of various magazines—but they've also compiled an archive of articles from their clients' publications, which you can search by topic. Note that this electronic news site also serves as a promotional site for some magazines and their subscription services.

Pathfinder (www.pathfinder. com) is the home page for Time Warner's periodicals, including *Time, People, Sports Illustrated,* and others. Choose a particular magazine or search the entire Pathfinder site for full-text articles from the entire Time Warner magazine group.

TV news giant **CNN** (www.cnn.com/SEARCH) provides text and pictures of current news events on its home page, as well as a search feature to find full-text articles in the news archives.

Another freebie, **InfoBeat, Inc.** (www.infobeat.com) delivers current news on topics you select, at the times you've requested, right to your current e-mail address. You can choose from finance, sports, news, entertainment, and other topics.

Online Databases

Serving up the best bibliography for the buck is **Electric Library** (www.elibrary.com). At this site, you'll find more than 150 full-text newspapers, several wire services, hundreds of full-text magazines, and references like *Collier's Encyclopedia* and *World Fact Book*. Though it's advertised as a general reference source for school and home users, it's also a viable and inexpensive resource for writers.

Rather than calling up a specific reference, you type in key words or a question or phrase relating to your topic on the **Electric Library Home Page.** After entering your search, results are returned to you ranked in order of relevance, listing source, author, and date of publication. Built-in intelligent search technology assures most of the results will be on target. Choose the documents you want, then print them or save them on disk. There's no limit or per-document charge. Best of all, there's a 30-day free trial.

CARLweb (www.carl.org) is a Web-based search interface for searching Knight-Ridder's huge inventory of articles, and it also acts as a link to other commercial databases. Their open access service provides free searches, which list the source, publication date, and a short summary of the content. You can order the full text from Carl for a nominal fee, or you can take your search results and look up articles yourself for free at the library.

Finding phone numbers and addresses of people and organizations can sometimes be a hassle, but there are several free databases that can help. If they're listed in any phone book, you'll find them at one of the following sites.

Database America (www.databaseamerica.com) gives one of the more comprehensive listings of residential phone numbers and addresses. You can search by either name, address, or phone number.

WhoWhere (www.whowhere. lycos.com) provides links to domestic phone directories, e-mail addresses, and personal Web pages.

Big Yellow (www.bigyellow. com) is the Internet's business yellow pages. You can search 16.5 million business listings by category or by specific names and addresses. There are also links to international directories.

WorldPages (www.world pages.com) combine white- and yellow-page listings, government listings, and links to 200 directories worldwide.

So how do you find out who's who? The A&E cable network sponsors **Biography** (www. biography.com). This spin-off of the popular TV program offers a searchable database of more than 15,000 people worth knowing, both past and present.

Writers and Writing Tools

The Internet has dozens of pages that cater to writers and journalists. Many provide research tips and sources, as well as specific information about the writing craft and the business of writing.

Several individuals have compiled lists of writers' resource links to various websites. Their content ranges from lists of reference resources on the Web to online writers' workshops. Since these lists change frequently, be sure to visit any or all of these sites on a regular basis. They include **Write.ms** (www.poewar. com) and **Writer Resources** (www. for writers.com).

Is it okay to join independent clauses with a comma? How can I write clearer, tighter sentences? **Strunk's Elements of Style** (www.bartleby.com) teaches beginners the tricks of clear and simple writing—and it's not a bad reference for experienced writers as well. This timeless 1918 version is still the standard for English usage.

The Home Researcher

"Don't leave home without it" was a catch phrase of the '80s that applied to a major credit card and applies equally to the researcher's library card. With the electronic research tools of today, you may not have to leave home at all. Instead, you can save precious time and effort gathering hard-to-find facts by using your computer as a research tool. For nearly the same cost as a year's worth of cable TV service, you can have unlimited Internet access for a year and a home CD-ROM reference library. ■

References:

In Print & Online

By Mark Haverstock

This comprehensive catalogue of references covers print and Internet versions of works writers can use to begin and to extend their research. Several of the online sites offer free services; others are fee-based or may be available to patrons at public or university libraries.

Note that websites and links are subject to change. If a website or link is unavailable, try using a major search engine to search for the site.

General References

Here you can begin your search for books or periodicals on any topic. You can also check to see if an idea you have for a book has already been done and, if so, how long ago.

■ **Amazon.com** and **Barnes & Noble**
www.amazon.com
www.bn.com

Both commercial bookseller websites offer a free, easily accessible alternative to *Books in Print*. Each can be searched by author, title, and many entries provide brief synopses or reviews.

■ **Books in Print**
www.booksinprint.com
New York, NY: R.R. Bowker, 1948-, annual. Listings from more than 49,000 publishers of their books currently in print. The multivolume set can be

searched by author or title.

In the Books in Print family are *Forthcoming Books* (bimonthly, 1966 -), *Paperbound Books in Print,* and *Books in Series.*

– *Subject Guide to Books in Print*

Books listed in *Books in Print* are assigned topical headings in this companion set. Contains nonfiction only. After your public library's catalogue, this is usually the next stop in an initial search for information. Indispensable for the writer.

– *Children's Books in Print*

New York, NY: R.R. Bowker, 1969-, annual. Following the same format as *Books in Print,* this reference lists over 88,000 books for children by author, title, and illustrator. It also contains information on 50 children's book awards: qualifications, past winners and when the award was established. A companion publication is the *Subject Guide to Children's Books in Print.* All of the *Books in Print* publications can be searched through online databases such as DIALOG and BRS or CD-ROM; ask if your library subscribes to these services. The website www.booksinprint.com combines all the *Books in Print* family as a paid online service with a free trial period. It includes these new features:

– *Bowker's Hooks to Holdings* allows libraries with Z39.50 compliant catalogues to let their professionals and patrons search the library's catalogue directly from booksinprint.com. Librarians and patrons can determine the availability and location of books already in the library's collection.

– *The Children's Room* lets you research, explore, and access every children's and young adult book, audiocassette, and video title in the database. In addition to the usual searches by author, illustrator, title, and subject, you can search by age, grade, or Lexile level, as well as by fictitious characters, imaginary settings, awards, reviews in 22 authoritative sources, and much more.

– *The Forthcoming Book Room* allows users to search for books, audiocassettes, and videos released during the current month or due to be published in the next six months.

■ **Children's Catalogue**

New York: H.W. Wilson, 1909-, annual supplements, cumulated. Lists books by Dewey number, with a bibliographic citation (including price, grade level, description, and evaluation). Includes indexes and directory of publishers.

■ **Cumulative Book Index**
www.hwwilson.com

New York: H.W. Wilson, 1898- monthly except August, cumulated. English language books by author, title, subject. Especially helpful for writers who want to find books on any given subject, including fiction titles on that topic. Both the Children's Catalogue and Cumulative Book Index are available in CD-ROM format on a subscription basis or online at WilsonWeb with free trial.

- ■ **Ulrich's International Periodicals Directory**
  www.ulrichsweb.com
  New York, NY: R.R. Bowker, 1932-, annual (with updates 2/year). Provides bibliographic information on over 165,000 periodicals classified under 69 subjects, with subject cross-referencing and index. Includes serials available on CD-ROM and online, cessations, refereed serials (reviewed by an expert in the field). Ulrich's Hotline helps subscribers in solving research problems.

- ■ **Readers' Guide to Periodical Literature**
  www.hwwilson.com
  New York: H. W. Wilson, 1901- monthly with annual cumulation. An author and subject index to approximately 250 selected general interest periodicals. For specialized research, try some of

the other Wilson guides, such as *Art Index, Social Sciences Index, Applied Science,* and *Technology Index.* Ask at the reference desk for these and many other specific subject indexes. *Readers' Guide* is available online as WilsonWeb on a subscription basis with free trial or in CD-ROM format.

Databases
Librarians at university and large public libraries can search national online services, which are collections of databases, saving you hundreds of hours of research time. Ask what is available, as there is usually a charge. Many libraries also now have databases for searching periodical information; a popular one is InfoTrac. Yours may also have CD-ROM encyclopedias and other research tools (many of the titles in this chapter are available on CD-ROM). For more information on databases and CD-ROMs, see *Gale Directory of Databases* (Detroit: Gale Research, every 6 months) and *CD-ROMs in Print* (Westport, CT: Meckler, annual).

Trade and Market Information
With these books you can target your article and book submissions, find an agent or a publisher, and keep up-to-date on books and news in the publishing world. Check your library, too, for specialty market guides

(for example, *Religious Writers Marketplace*) by subject or region.

■ Writer's Market

www.writersmarket.com

Cincinnati: Writer's Digest Books, annual. A practical, comprehensive guide to the business side of writing. Lists book and magazine publishers with editors' names, what they are looking for, intended audience, submission guidelines, and how to obtain sample copies and writers' guidelines. Script, syndicate, and greeting card markets are also covered, as well as basic information on queries, manuscript format, rights, taxes. *Writer's Market Electronic Edition* is sold with book and accompanying CD-ROM.

Other titles of interest from Writer's Digest Books are:

–Children's Writer's & Illustrator's Market: Follows the same format as *Writer's Market,* including articles specifically aimed to inform and inspire the writer for children.

– Novel & Short Story Writer's Market: Follows the same format as *Writer's Market,* but created exclusively for fiction writers, it provides every fiction market, plus agents, articles, contests, and organizations.

■ The Writer's Handbook

Edited by Sylvia K. Burack.

Boston: *The Writer,* annual. The first half of the book contains articles by authors about writing. The second half has lists of markets, how to contact, what they publish, number of words, pay, more. Lists a variety of magazines, book publishers, theaters, conferences, writers' colonies.

■ Literary Market Place (LMP)

www.literarymarketplace.com

New York, NY: R.R. Bowker, annual. Contains a wealth of information about the publishing industry. Check this if you need to find a certain type of publisher, help with photo research, public relations and promotion, an agent, proofreader, consultant, or contest. More than 2,000 pages of the names and addresses of anyone having anything to do with books.

Related titles are:

–International Literary Marketplace New Providence, MJ: R.R. Bowker, 1983- , annual. (Also available on CD-ROM.) This publication provides information similar to that provided in *Literary Market Place,* but on an international scale. It lists publishers in more than 160 countries, identifies major international booksellers and libraries, and provides other international publishing information. Some free services are available online for registered users.

- **The Insider's Guide to Book Editors, Publishers, & Literary Agents, 2001-2002**
Jeff Herman. Rocklin, CA: Prima, 1999. Lists publishers' addresses, phone numbers, contact names, and what they publish. Also includes articles on writing and lists of organizations.

- **International Directory of Little Magazines and Small Presses**
Len Fulton, ed. New York: Pushcart Press, annual. A listing of alternative, literary, and small press offerings. Companion volume: *Directory of Small Press & Magazine Editors & Publishers,* the name index to title above.

- **Publishers Weekly**
www.publishersweekly.com
New York: R.R. Bowker, 1872-, weekly. The magazine to read for information on the publishing world. See especially the spring and fall children's book announcement issues.

- **Booklist**
www.ala.org/booklist/index.html
Chicago: American Library Association, 1905-, 22/year. Index plus selected features and reviews from past issues available online.

- **The Horn Book Magazine**
www.hbook.com/mag.shtml
Boston: *Horn Book Magazine,* 1925-bimonthly. The magazine is a standard in the children's literature field. The magazine has published a semiannual *Horn Book Guide* since 1989. On the website are a virtual history exhibit and some archived features and reviews.

- **School Library Journal**
www.slj.com
New York: School Library Journal. 1954-, monthly. Features, columns, and useful news.

Biography
People are the primary makers of history and libraries are full of biographical sources. Whether all you need are birth and death dates, or a whole book about a famous person, this section will guide you to your needed information. Historical and present-day sources overlap, although some are specifically about one or the other.

- **Biography.com**
www.biography.com
The website of the Biography channel on cable television, Biography.com contains a comprehensive list of historical figures and celebrities, along with brief biographies. It includes web pages for teachers, discussions, and more.

- **Biography and Genealogy Master Index**

2nd ed. Detroit: Gale Research, 1980. 8 volumes. With annual updates, cumulated every five years. Original set contains 3.2 million citations to articles in standard works of collective biography; updates add thousands more each year. Biographical sources fill many shelves; start here to save time. Arranged by person's last name, followed by biographical sources person appears in. Online version available at libraries.

- **Biography Index**

www.hwwilson.com

New York: H. W. Wilson, 1947- , quarterly, cumulated (now annually). Indexes biographical material, whether magazine, book, or chapter in a book, by name of subject. Also available on CD-ROM or online as WilsonWeb or on a subscription basis with free trial.

- **Who's Who**

New York, NY: Marquis *Who's Who.* Publishes many titles, including *Who's Who,* 1849- , annual; *Who's Who in America,* 1899- , annual; *Who Was Who,* 1897- ; *Who Was Who in America,* 1897-; *Who Was Who in America Historical Volume, 1607-1896; Marquis Who's Who Publications: Index to all Books,* 1974- , bienni-

al. Also available in CD-ROM and online through LEXIS-NEXIS.

- **The International Who's Who**

London: Europa Publications, 1935-, annual. Short biographies of almost 20,000 living persons with dates, career, publications, interests, address, and phone. Also available on CD-ROM.

- **Almanac of Famous People**

5th ed. Detroit: Gale Research, 1994. Brief biographical sketches of 27,000 persons, living and dead. Alphabetical by name, with indexes.

- **Current Biography Yearbook**

www.hwwilson.com

New York: H.W. Wilson 1940- , monthly except December, cumulated annually. Long articles (several pages) of current persons of note, with biographical references at end. Also available in CD-ROM format and online, as WilsonWeb or on a subscription basis with free trial.

- **Biography Today**

Detroit, MI: Omnigraphics, Inc. 1992- , three times yearly, cumulated annually. Profiles of contemporary people of interest to young readers.

- **Newsmakers**

Detroit: Gale Research, 1988-,

quarterly, with annual cumulation (supersedes Contemporary Newsmakers, 1985-87). Up-to-date biographical and career profiles of people in the news. Covers all fields, from business and international affairs to literature and the arts.

■ **The Dictionary of National Biography**

Founded in 1882 by George Smith. London: Oxford University 1908-9. Twenty-two volumes and nine supplements cover Britain's citizens from "earliest times" to 1900, including noteworthy colonial Americans. Evaluative and factual information.

■ **Dictionary of American Biography**

American Council of Learned Societies. New York: Charles Scribner's Sons, 1928-36, ongoing. 20 volumes, index volume,and supplement volumes with comprehensive index. Similar to the *Dictionary of National Biography*; presents lives of now dead Americans through essays by people who knew them. Also available in CD-ROM.

■ **The National Cyclopaedia of American Biography**

New York: James T. White, 1898- . Biographies of living and dead Americans. Not in alphabetical order, but each volume has an index and a cumulative index was published in 1984.

■ **Notable Americans: What They Did, from 1620 to the Present**

4th ed. Edited by Linda S. Hubbard. Detroit: Gale Research, 1988. Listing of names only. Includes candidates in presidential elections, members of Congress (including in the Confederacy), mayors, association executives, award winners, more.

■ **Research Guide to American Historical Biography**

Edited by Robert Muccigrosso. Washington, DC: Beacham, 1988-91. 3 volumes. Biographies of 278 famous Americans, followed by a listing of primary sources, fiction, juvenile biographies, archives, museums, societies devoted to the person.

■ **Biographical Directory of the American Congress 1774-1971**

bioguide.congress.gov

Washington, DC: U.S. Government Printing Office, 1971. First part arranged chronologically by each Congress, including the Continental Congress; lists senators and representatives from each state and territory. Second part is arranged alphabetically by name; short biography.

■ **Notable American Women 1607-1950: A Biographical Dictionary**
Edited by Edward T. James. Cambridge, MA: Belknap Press of Harvard University Press, 1971. 3 volumes. Encyclopedic articles, with further reference sources at end.

■ **Notable American Women, the Modern Period**
Edited by Barbara Sicherman and Carol Hurd Green. Cambridge, MA: Belknap Press of Harvard University Press, 1980. 442 biographies, covering the late nineteenth- to the mid-twentieth centuries.

■ **Contemporary Black Biography**
Detroit: Gale Research, 1992- . 9 volumes as of 1995. Includes biographical and interview information, photographs, writings, awards, and sources. Most of the subjects are modern, although some are from earlier in the twentieth century.

■ **Encyclopedia of Frontier Biography**
Dan L. Thrapp. Lincoln: University of Nebraska Press.

Short biographies of explorers, Indians, soldiers, outlaws, scouts, hunters, artists, and more. References for further reading under each entry. Also available on CD-ROM.

■ **American Historical Images on File: The Faces of America**
New York: Facts on File, 1990. Portrait (large photo, drawing, engraving, painting) of subject with short biography. Artists, statesmen, musicians, sports figures, explorers, industrialists, journalists, many more. See also others in this series: *The Black Experience, Colonial and Revolutionary America, The Native American Experience,* and others.

■ **Corbis**
www.corbis.com
Commercial site containing vast collection of photos, incorporating Bettmann Archive. Portraits of artists, statesmen, musicians, sports figures, explorers, industrialists, journalists, many more. Thumbnail views available; pictures downloadable.

■ **Eponyms Dictionaries Index**
Detroit: Gale Research, 1977, with 1984 supplement. Where did Graham crackers, Ferris wheel, and the Taft-Hartley Act get their names? Find out here. Identifies biographical sources

and dictionaries for 33,000 eponymous terms.

History

Read a newspaper article from the 1800s, a speech delivered in 1961, or an eyewitness account of a Colonial event. For writers of historical fiction and nonfiction, here is a guide to an exciting trip back in time. Included are general works, chronologies, and historical indexes; check out your library's reference works for histories of specific ethnic groups, countries, and fields of knowledge.

■ **World History: A Dictionary of Important People, Places, and Events, from Ancient Times to the Present**
Bruce Wetterau. New York: Henry Holt, 1995. Short entries on almost 10,000 subjects, plus chronologies.

■ **The Encyclopedia of World Facts and Dates**
Gorton Carruth. New York: Harper-Collins, 1993. In chronological order, from the Big Bang 18 billion years ago to 1992. Covers all areas.

■ **The New York Public Library Book of Chronologies**
Bruce Wetterau. New York: Prentice-Hall, 1990. Differs from other books of this type in its arrangement by subject (more than 250 separate chronologies).

■ **The Timetables of History**
3rd rev. Bernard Grun. New York: Simon & Schuster, 1991. Follow tables from 5000 B.C. to the present to see what events occurred at the same time in history/politics, literature/theater, religion/philosophy, visual arts, music, science/technology, and daily life.

■ **Day by Day: the Eighties**
Edited by Ellen Metzler, Marc Aronson. New York: Facts on File, 1995. World events, U.S. politics and economy, science/technology, culture/leisure is listed for each month and day of decades from the 1940s to the 1980s.

■ **Chronicle of the 20th Century**
Liberty, MO: JL International Publishing, 1992. Each page represents one month of each year from 1900 on; short articles on what happened in all areas. See also *Chronicle of the World, America, French Revolution, Second World War,* and other titles by the same publisher.

■ **Chronicle of the 20th Century**
Dorling Kindersley, 1996. This book, with the same title as the preceding but from a differ-

ent publisher, has full-color photographs, a simple and concise text, and a newspaper-style format to report the major events and people of the century, from world wars to the technological explosion. Also available in CD-ROM format.

■ **Monarchs, Rulers, Dynasties, and Kingdoms of the World**
Compiled by R.F. Tapsell. New York: Facts on File, 1983. Lists over 13,000 rulers and dynasties by country in chronological order.

■ **International Dictionary of Historic Places**
Chicago: Fitzroy Dearborn, 1995. 5 volumes: Americas, Northern Europe, Southern Europe, Middle East and Africa, Asia and Oceania. Several pages for each place, such as Boston's Freedom Trail, Hollywood, Santiago.

■ **Dictionary of Historic Documents**
George C. Kohn. New York: Facts on File, 1991. Short explanations of more than 2,200 documents, including Code of Hammurabi, Ten Commandments, U.S. Pledge of Allegiance, Treaty of Paris, Cuban Constitution; with dates.

■ **The Annals of America**
Chicago: Encyclopaedia Britannica, 1976. 20 volumes plus supplement volume 21 (1987). Speeches, letters, diaries, poems, book and magazine excerpts, songs, pictures, and background on important issues in American life by famous and little-known authors.

■ **The Annals of the Civil War**
Cambridge, MA: Da Capo Press, 1994. 1878 volume is essentially a massive collection of eyewitness accounts of the Civil War. Besides battle scenes, the annals also cover the draft riots in New York and prisoner-of-war recollections.

■ **Documents of American History**
10th ed. Edited by Henry Steele Cormmager and Milton Cantor. Englewood Cliffs, NJ: Prentice-Hall, 1988. 2 volumes. Includes proclamations, acts, decrees, decisions, speeches from 1492 to the present; collected by a noted historian.

■ **Historical Statistics of the United States: Colonial Times to 1970**
White Plains, NY: Kraus International Publications, prepared by Bureau of the Census, 1989. 2 volumes. Need to know the population in 1790? Facts about immigrants in 1820? Exports in the 1600s? This refer-

ence has those numbers and much more. Available on CD-ROM.

■ **Famous First Facts**

4th ed. Joseph Nathan Kane. New York: LW. Wilson, 1981. Lists more than 9,000 first happenings in American history from 1007 A.D. to 1980. Alphabetical by fact, with extensive indexing.

■ **This Day in American History**

Ernie Gross. New York: Neal Schuman, 1990. 11,000 entries under day of the year they happened.

■ **This Day in History**

www.historychannel.com/thisday

Website sponsored by History Channel. Gives summary of historical events for current date or date of your choice.

■ **The Negro Almanac: A Reference Work on the African American**

5th ed. Compiled and edited by Harry A. Ploski and James Williams. Detroit: Gale Research, 1989. Comprehensive overview of black culture, with statistics, biographies, chronologies, and articles on legal, historic, labor, political, artistic, religious areas. 1,600+ pages.

■ **The Writer's Guide to Everyday Life in the 1800s**

Marc McCutcheon. Cincinnati: Writer's Digest Books, 1993. Covers clothing, language, transportation, furniture, money, medicine, dances, foods, crime, war. Includes chronologies of events, books, magazines, innovations, songs. See also *The Writer's Guide to Everyday Life: Prohibition to World War II,* by the same author (1995) and *The Writer's Guide to Everyday Life in the Middle Ages,* by Sherrilyn Kenyon (1995) and *The Writer's Guide to Everyday Life in the Renaissance,* by Kathy Lynn Emerson.

■ **Poole's Index to Periodical Literature, 1802-1906**

William Frederick Poole. Boston: Houghton Mifflin, 1882-1908. 2 volumes plus supplements. Helpful for the writer who wants to examine style of writing or read original texts from the nineteenth and early twentieth-century. *Author Index,* compiled by C. Edward Wall. Michigan: Pierian Press. Cumulative, 1971.

■ **Famous First Facts About the States**

David Stienecker. Woodbridge, CT: Blackbirch Press, 1995. Gives information on state birds, flowers, and trees, for all 50 states, along with notes on famous people born in each state and important dates in state history.

Local History Sources

To find out how the people of your community lived in the past and what events affected their lives, look for old newspapers, genealogies, and local history books of the era. Ask your librarian how to access these sources; some major libraries have sizable genealogy and local history collections.

■ **United States Local Histories in the Library of Congress: Bibliography**
Edited by Marion J. Kaminkow. Baltimore: Magna Carta, 1975. 4 volumes, 1 supplement (1986) with index. Arranged by region, then state. Includes city, title, place, publisher, date, number of pages. After you find the titles, you may be able to find these locally or through interlibrary loan.

News Sources

From current events reporting comes story ideas, people to contact for information and interviews, and the very latest in what's happening in any field. Back issues and volumes can be handy, too, for historical perspective.

■ **Facts on File: World News Digest with Index**
www.facts.com
New York: Facts on File, 1941-, weekly with bound annual cumulation. Cumulative index issued every two months. Condenses the news of the week from more than 70 newspapers and newsmagazines around the world. Includes fact boxes, references to earlier articles, maps, tables. Covers government/politics, health, economy/finance, the arts, sports, environment, national/international events, business, science. Includes a color world atlas with index. CD-ROM available quarterly, cumulated annually. Available on the Web as a subscription service, with a free trial.

■ **The CQ Researcher**
www.cq.com
(Formerly Editorial Research Reports). Washington, DC: Congressional Quarterly, 1923- , weekly. Each volume addresses one topic, such as organ transplants. Includes background, current views, the future, sources for more information, and subject and title indexes. Subscriber website.

■ **Newspapers in Microform, United States and Newspapers in Microform, Foreign Countries**
Washington, DC: Library of Congress, 1984. Covers 1948-1983. By state, city, with title index. Lists hundreds of libraries. Dates of publication and title changes helpful for researcher.

- **NewsBank**
  www.newsbank.com
  New Canaan, CT: NewsBank, 1981-monthly, with quarterly and annual cumulations. Provides subject access to articles from newspapers of more than 450 U.S. cities. Full text is on microfiche, index is printed. Has direction for use on each page. Searchable version, NewsBank Infoweb, available to subscribing schools and libraries.

Major Newspaper Indexes

The following newspaper indexes are in most large public libraries and are also available on CD-ROM. Searchable archives are available on the Internet, but may only include issues from recent years. Some may also charge fee for full-text downloads.

- **The New York Times Index**
  archives.nytimes.com
  1851-, semi-monthly.

- **Wall Street Journal Index**
  interactive.wsj.com
  1955-, monthly.

- **Washington Post Index**
  www.washingtonpost.com
  1971- , monthly.

- **USA Today Web Archives**
  www.usatoday.com
  1988- .

- **General Periodical Searches**
  The following websites offer a variety of full-text downloads from major periodicals. All provide article summaries and free search. They are fee-based and charge either flat access fee or per article.

- **Northern Light**
  www.northernlight.com
- **Electric Library**
  www.elibrary.com

Literature and Legend

Literature in general and children's literature in particular benefit from a good number of reference books. Specialized indexes abound to find poetry, essays, fairy tales, plays, songs, short stories, speeches, and book reviews.

- **The Oxford Companion to Children's Literature**
  Humphrey Carpenter and Mari Prichard. Oxford: Oxford University Press, 1984. Alphabetical listing of authors, characters, categories of children's literature, titles, and geographical areas (children's literature in various countries).

- **Characters from Young Adult Literature**
  Mary Ellen Snodgrass. Englewood, CO: Libraries Unlimited, 1991. Settings, syn-

opsis, major and minor characters for each work, with author and character indexes.

■ **Oxford Dictionary of Nursery Rhymes**
Edited by Iona and Peter Opie. London: Oxford University Press, 1984. Arranged alphabetically by most prominent word (cat, father, London Bridge); gives origin and explanation.

■ **Calendar of Literary Facts**
Edited by Samuel J. Rogal. Detroit: Gale Research, 1991. Day-by-day: births and deaths of famous authors, publishers. By year: births, deaths, publications, events.

■ **Pseudonyms and Nicknames Dictionary**
Edited by Jennifer Mossman. Detroit: Gale Research, 1987. 2 volumes. 80,000 aliases, pen names, code names, stage names, etc., of 55,000 persons; provides real name, basic biographical information, and sources. Covers many fields.

■ **Brewer's Dictionary of Names**
Adrian Room. New York: Cassell, 1992. Defines people, places, and things in mythology, the Bible, history, politics, business, languages, literature, astronomy.

■ **Children's Writer's Word Book**
Alijandra Mogilner. Cincinnati, OH: Writer's Digest Books, 1992. Word lists by grade and a thesaurus using graded words.

■ **The Macmillan Visual Dictionary**
New York: Macmillan, 1995. Labels parts of objects such as tape measure, bulldozer, camera, baseball field, snake; names and shows types of glassware, tools, road signs, dresses, furniture. 25,000 terms in 600 subjects. A multilingual edition is also available.

■ **YourDictionary.com**
www.yourdictionary.com
Originally named *The Web of Online Dictionaries,* this site was launched in 1995 by Dr. Robert Beard at Bucknell University as a research tool for the world's linguistic community. This comprehensive Web portal specializes in information about any language. Look up a general or specialized word in English or foreign-language dictionaries.

■ **The Oxford English Dictionary**
2nd ed. Oxford: Clarendon, 1989. 20 volumes. First choice for looking up pronunciation, meaning, and historical origin of any word. For writers: Find out if

an object, phrase, or word was used in the year you are writing about.

■ Random House Historical Dictionary of American Slang

Volume 1, A-G. Edited by J.E. Lighter. New York: Random House, 1994. Well-received first volume of proposed multivolume set. Includes when slang was first used, with year, author, and reference (can be book, magazine, television show, film). Usually several examples of usage under each word.

■ The Macmillan Book of Proverbs, Maxims, and Famous Phrases

Selected and arranged by Burton Stevenson. New York: Macmillan, 1987. Nearly 3,000 pages; traces sources (title, author, date). Arranged by subject, with index.

■ A Dictionary of American Proverbs

Edited by Stewart A. Kingsbury and Kelsie B. Harder. New York: Oxford University Press, 1992. Organized according to word; reveals the proverb source (first use and in the twentieth century) and distribution (by state).

■ The Dictionary of Phrase and Fable

www.bibliomania.com/ Reference/
PhraseAndFable/index.html
This classic work of reference by E. Cobham Brewer has been in popular demand since 1870. The dictionary is extensively cross referenced, listing terms and characters that appear in classic literature. This First Hypertext Edition is taken from Dr. Brewer's substantially revised and extended edition of 1894.

■ Bartlett's Familiar Quotations

www.bartleby.com
16th ed. Edited by Justin Kaplan. Boston: Little, Brown, and Company, 1992. Arranged in chronological order, with indexes by author and quote. Version also available on the Internet: It's the 9th Edition, copyright 1901, but still an excellent resource.

■ The Quotations Page

www.starlingtech.com/quotes/
This page was originally developed as a catalogue of quotation resources on the Internet; it has since evolved into a large-scale quotation site with many original resources. Also contains numerous links to other quotation sites.

A Dictionary of Common Fallacies

Philip Ward. Buffalo, NY: Prometheus, 1988. 2 volumes. Find out why mermaids don't exist, whales don't spout water, and the Declaration of Independence was not signed on July 4, 1776, and why so many people believe it was.

Bulfinch's Mythology

www.bulfinch.org

Edited by Richard P. Martin. New York: Modern Library, 1991. The classic in its field. Includes gods and goddesses (including Hindu and Norse), King Arthur and knights, other British hero tales, Charlemagne legends.

Encyclopedia Mythica

www.pantheon.org/mythica

This is an encyclopedia on mythology, folklore, legends, and more. It contains over 5,700 definitions of gods and goddesses, supernatural beings and legendary creatures and monsters from all over the world.

Funk and Wagnalls Standard Dictionary of Folklore, Mythology and Legend

Edited by Maria Leach. San Francisco: Harper & Row, 1984. More than 8,000 articles (some long, some short) on folk heroes, beliefs, spells, rhymes, festivals, dances, more.

Science

Information about science and technology is available at many levels of depth and difficulty. Investigate until you find the sources most comfortable for you.

McGraw-Hill Encyclopedia of Science & Technology

7th ed. New York: McGraw-Hill, 1992. 20 volumes. 7,500 entries, 13,000 illustrations, analytical index, topical index, cross-references, study guides, list of contributing authors. CD-ROM and online versions available.

McGraw-Hill Dictionary of Scientific and Technical Terms

5th ed. Edited by Sybil P. Parker. New York: McGraw-Hill, 1994. Includes pronunciation, field or subject, short definition. Handy appendices.

Dictionary of Scientific Literacy

Richard P. Brennan. New York: John Wiley & Sons, 1992. Short explanation of words and phrases the average adult needs to know, from absolute zero to zygote with Doppler effect, global warming, radio telescope, much more.

Chemical Formulary

New York: Chemical Publishing, 1933- . Ongoing multivolume set contains formulas for foods, drugs, cosmetics, cleaners, fabrics, adhesives, more. Good especially for historical research. *Cumulative Index* to volumes 1-25. Harry Bennett. New York: Chemical Publishing, 1987.

■ **Milestones in Science and Technology: The Ready Reference Guide to Discoveries, Inventions, and Facts**
2nd ed. Ellis Mount and Barbara A. List. Phoenix, AZ: Oryx, 1994. 1,250 topics such as gasoline, rocket, porcelain, cable TV, zipper; includes explanation, field, and suggested reading.

■ **Asimov's Chronology of Science & Discovery**
Isaac Asimov. New York: HarperCollins, 1994. Asimov died in 1992, but his name lives on in this updated version of one of his many books. From 4,000,000 B.C. to 1993 what was happening in math, medicine, technology, astronomy, agriculture, exploration, and more. Easy to understand.

■ **The Timetables of Technology**
Bryan Bunch and Alexander Hellemans. New York: Simon & Schuster, 1993. Follow the advance of invention, discovery, publications, construction from 2,400,000 B.C. to the present in tables. See also *The Timetables of*

Science, by the same authors.

■ **McGraw-Hill Yearbook of Science & Technology**
New York: McGraw-Hill, 1962-, annual. Supplement to the McGraw-Hill Encyclopedia of Science and Technology. Articles from AIDS to zeolite on the achievements in science and engineering, with charts, diagrams, graphs, photos.

■ **Yearbook of Science and the Future**
Chicago: Encyclopaedia Britannica, 1975-, annual. Science update in the familiar *Encyclopaedia Brittanica* format, to revise certain sections of that work; year in review takes in all scientific fields; more.

Field Guides
Field guides cover all areas of science. They are very helpful for identification, geographical location, and description. Some examples:

■ **National Audubon Society Field Guide to African Wildlife**
Peter C. Alden. New York: Alfred A. Knopf, 1995.

■ **Simon & Schuster's Guide to Saltwater Fish and Fishing**
Angelo Mojetta. New, York: Simon & Schuster, 1992.

Almanacs

Almanacs include retrospective information and basic standard information, and are generally more up-to-date than encyclopedias. This list includes general American almanacs, international, and specialized subject almanacs. General almanacs contain look-it-up-fast info: yearly data such as members of Congress, current events, and sports statistics, and general information such as maps, text of the Constitution, facts on nations and states, outline of history, and so on. The following are some of the most popular.

■ **Information Please Almanac**
www.infoplease.com
Boston: Houghton Mifflin, 1947- , annual. Content also available on the website.

■ **The World Almanac and Book of Facts**
Mahwah, NJ: World Almanac Books, 1868-1876, 1886- annual.

■ **Canadian Almanac & Directory**
Toronto: Canadian Almanac & Directory Publishing, 1847- , annual. Provides geographical and political information. Lists hospitals, unions, organizations, television stations, magazines, publishers, libraries, museums.

■ **The Annual Register World Events: A Review of the Year**
New York: Stockton: 1758- , annual. Published in the U.K., copublished in U.S. and Canada. Country-by-country events and almanac-type information, international bodies (UN, NATO, African conferences, etc.), fields of religion, science, environment, architecture, arts, law, sports, more.

■ **Statesman's Year Book**
London: Macmillan/New York: St. Martin's, 1864-, annual. Bulk of the book is current information on countries (politics, economics, statistics, weather); small section on international organizations.

■ **Europa World Year Book**
London: Europa Publications, 1926- , annual since 1960. Provides detailed statistical and historical information about every country in the world.

■ **Demographic Yearbook**
www.un.org/popin
New York: United Nations, 1948-, annual. Compilations of statistics for over 200 countries, such as population, life expectancy, marriage, divorce, deaths. Some data available on United Nations Population Information Network (POPIN) at the Web address.

CIA World Fact Book

www.cia.gov/cia/publications/factbook/

This source of important unclassified CIA data covers the nations of the world, from Afghanistan to Zimbabwe—area, political climate, international disputes, natural resources, environment, population, inflation rate, GDP, agriculture, industries, defense expenditures, national holidays, literacy rate, religion, legal system, labor force, and much more, and includes a map for every entry. CD-ROM and print versions available.

Almanac of the 50 States: Basic Data Profiles with Comparative Tables

Edited by Edith R. Hornor. Palo Alto, CA: Information Publications, 1985- , State-by-state statistics: geography, demographics, vital statistics, education, government, economics, communications. Tables ranking states in area, population, education, labor force, income, more.

The Old Farmer's Almanac

www.almanac.com

Dublin, NH: Yankee Publishing, 1792- , annual. Astronomy, farmer's calendar, weather predictions, entertaining articles and useful information. Selected information available on the website.

The Weather Almanac

7th ed. Detroit: Gale Research, 1996. Historical and current U.S. information. Lots of statistics for each city, plus articles on weather, air, storms, with charts, maps, photographs.

Atlases

For a standard geographical/political atlas, look for a recent copyright date. Changes have been too fast the past few years to trust an old one. Beyond that, there are atlases on just about any subject—sports, caves, railroads, politics, women, etc. so browse your reference section! Historical atlases concentrate on the past and can be general or specific for countries or events. Gazetteers are dictionaries of geographical place names.

The International Atlas

Chicago: Rand McNally, 1993. Views of the world, from regions, countries, down to individual cities. Multilingual.

Hammond New Century World Atlas

Maplewood, NJ: Hammond, 1996. Contains political, physical, topical maps. Hammond Atlas of the World available on CD-ROM.

Atlas of the World

Washington, DC: National

Geographic Society, 1992, revised 6th edition. Includes infrared and satellite photos; the moon, the solar system, and a brief statistical overview of each country.

■ **The Times Atlas of the World**
9th ed. London: Times Books, 1992. Plates contain all types of maps, with easy-to-read key. Lists 210,000 place names in index.

■ **The Dorling-Kindersley World Reference Atlas**
London: Dorling-Kindersley, 1994. Colorful, country-by-country coverage. Maps, charts, graphs, statistics, world ranking, chronology, many facts.

■ **Microsoft Encarta World Atlas**
This CD-ROM based multimedia atlas contains over 1.7 million place names. Displays world music, flags and national anthems directly on the map. Informative new map "treks" explain key earth science topics like glaciers, volcanoes and deserts. The program offers 21 map styles, 11,000 articles and 6,500 images, videos, and audio files.

■ **The Economist Atlas of the New Europe**
New York: Henry Holt, 1992. Arranged by subject: history, communications, business, finance, politics, international relations, war, environment, people and culture, and, within each, by a country analysis. Big, colorful use of maps and charts.

■ **Atlas of Contemporary America: Portrait of a Nation**
Rodger Doyle. New York: Facts on File, 1994. Includes population density, ethnic dispersion, weather, taxes, political climate, much more.

■ **Atlas of United States Environmental Issues**
Robert J. Mason and Mark T. Mattson. New York: Macmillan, 1990. Maps, charts, and text used to illustrate water, waste, air, forest, energy, and other topics affecting the environment.

■ **The Rand-McNally Commercial Atlas and Marketing Guide**
Chicago: Rand McNally, annual. Need a map of railroads, military installations, or college population? This huge book is filled with statistics and maps. Provides population, economic, and geographical data for more than 128,000 U.S. places, with detailed maps.

■ **Ancient History Atlas**
Michael Grant. New York:

Macmillan, 1971. By the acclaimed historian. 87 very clear, easy-to-read maps cover 1700 B.C. to 500 A.D. in the ancient Greek and Roman world.

■ **The Times Atlas of World History**
Edited by Geoffrey Barraclough. Maplewood, NJ: Hammond, 1993. A visual and written narrative of world history from earliest times to the present. Detailed maps.

■ **Chambers World Gazetteer: An A-Z of Geographical Information**
5th ed. Edited by Dr. David Munro. Cambridge: Chambers, 1988. Place words (cities, countries, states, geographical sites) with pronunciation, location, information, sometimes a map.

■ **Omni Gazetteer of the United States of America**
Detroit: Omnigraphics, 1991. 11 volumes. Contains 1.5 million place names in the U.S. and its territories. Arranged by region, then by state, with an alphabetical list of places and information about each. Includes indexes. Also available on CD-ROM.

■ **The Map Catalogue.**
Edited by Joel Makower. 3rd ed.

New York, Vintage, 1992. Sourcebook of maps to purchase (historical, county, wildlife, weather, and others) plus aerial photographs, educational materials, anything connected to maps or geography.

■ **Freeality**
www.freeality.com/maps.htm
Collection of atlases, roadmaps, and driving directions. Site also contains other useful reference links.

Encyclopedias

Encyclopedias can be a good place to start a search, but they are almost never the place to end when writing for children. Editors of books and magazines alike today demand broader and deeper research for their readers. Encyclopedias as "sources of all knowledge" can be just one book or a multivolume set. For a review of various encyclopedias, see *Kister's Best Encyclopedias* (Phoenix: Oryx, 1994), where Kenneth Kister compares and evaluates general and specialized encyclopedias.

■ **Academic American Encyclopedia.**
Danbury, CT: Grolier

■ **Collier's Encyclopedia**
New York: P.F. Collier

- Compton's Encyclopedia
  Chicago: Compton's Learning/ Encyclopaedia Britannica

- Encyclopedia Americana
  Danbury, CT: Grolier

- The New Book of Knowledge
  Danbury, CT: Grolier

- New Encyclopaedia
  Britannica
  Chicago: Encyclopaedia Britannica

- World Book Encyclopedia
  Chicago: World Book

CD-ROM Encyclopedias:
- **Academic American**
- **Britannica**
- **Compton's**
- **Concise Columbia**
- **Funk and Wagnalls**
- **Grolier (Academic American Encyclopedia)**
- **Information Finder (World Book Encyclopedia)**
- **Microsoft Encarta**
- **Random House**

Encyclopedia Websites
- www.encyclopedia.com
  The Concise Columbia Electronic Encyclopedia, Third Edition

- www.britannica.com
  Encyclopaedia   Britannica encarta.msn.com   (Microsoft Encarta)

- www.redesk.com/myency.html
  My Virtual Encyclopedia

Subject encyclopedias:
Choose from dozens available at your local library. Just a quick scan of the shelves can lead you to encyclopedias on computer science, comics, crime, cities, states, science fiction, mammals, medicine, music, art, antiques, espionage, extraterrestrials, the Renaissance, religions, Western lawmen, and world coins. The following are examples of two multivolume sets that are worth checking.

- Oxford Illustrated Encyclopedia
  New York: Oxford University Press, 1993. 8 volumes: 1. The Physical World. 2. The Natural World. 3. World History from Earliest Times to 1800. 4. World History from 1800 to the Present Day. 5. The Arts. 6. Invention and   Technology.   7.   The Universe.   8.   Peoples   and Culture. Edited by experts in each field; sumptuous illustrations.

- World Geographical Encyclopedia
  New   York: McGraw-Hill, 1995. 5 volumes: 1. Africa. 2. The Americas. 3. Asia. 4. Europe. 5. Oceania and index. Geography, history, economics, and the pol-

itics of each country, plus beautiful color photos.

Government Documents
The U.S. government, the largest publisher in the world, is a source of information that all writers should keep in mind when beginning their research. If you can think of a subject, the government has probably published a book, pamphlet, periodical, or statistic about it.

■ **Monthly Catalogue of U.S. Government Publications**
Washington, DC: U.S. Government Printing Office, 1895- , monthly, with supplements, cumulations, and indexes. All branches, agencies, and departments are represented in this up-to-date list.

■ **Statistical Abstract of the United States**
Washington, DC: U.S. Department of Commerce, Bureau of the Census, 1878-, annual. More than just population numbers; for example, attendance for various arts activities by sex, race, age, education level, and income, or average annual expenditure on consumer goods by region and size of household. If you need numbers, look here first.

■ **The United States Government Manual**
Washington, DC: Office of the Federal Register, National Archives and Administration, General Services, annual. Lists names and addresses of government offices and their head people. ■

Libraries Online:
Content, Not Catalogues

By Mary Northrup

Remember when the World Wide Web was new and we were promised we would have the libraries of the world at our fingertips? Well, we can now connect to almost any library, but for the most part what we get is that library's catalogue. While this is very handy for the researcher who wants to know what's available, sometimes we want content, not a catalogue.

Yet some library websites deliver great content: literary texts, historical images, primary documents, maps, music, ads, and much more. Writers who research will be delighted with the treasures that await—with no need to travel.

The scope of these sites is wide, encompassing many subjects, although history is especially strong. Sample the sites listed below, then do your own searching. For local history, check out the websites of libraries in the geographical area you are researching. Many have digital collections of texts and photos highlighting their region. Because the information is provided through a university or public library, it's accuracy should be extremely high.

While researchers will always need to search out books, articles, memorabilia, and actual physical locations, more and more texts and images will show up on websites. What better place to find these than in online libraries?

■ **The Library of Congress**
www.lcweb.loc.gov

Just as our national library in Washington, DC, takes up an enormous amount of physical space, its presence on the Web is huge. In user-friendly format, the home page offers a tempting variety of information.

Click on American Memory, and you have access to more than five million items available for viewing, including such highlights as baseball cards of 1887 to 1914, folk music from Depression-era migrant worker camps, the papers of Alexander Graham Bell in his own writing, quilts and interviews with quilt-makers in America in the last 20 years, women's rights tracts from the National American Woman Suffrage Association of 1848 to 1921, and maps of the national parks. Browse through pamphlets, manuscripts, audio and video clips, letters, photographs, sheet music, portraits, and documents from all eras of American history. The collections are well-organized and searchable by keyword, topic, original format, or time period. This is a treasure trove for the researcher in Americana.

Go to *Exhibitions: An On-line Gallery* to find out about feature attractions at the Library of Congress. Even if you can't travel, you can gather much information at this site as you revel in the variety of cultural artifacts contained here.

The Library Today is an up-to-date collection of news and special events going on at the Library of Congress. Again, much information is available for the person who can access only through the Web. One sample day featured news of an online author chat; an announcement of a new exhibition about Chautauqua, New York, a historical center where artistic festivals, seminars, and events take place; a long, illustrated article about James Madison; a report, including a Web cast, on the New Digital Reference Service organized by the Library of Congress and other libraries; and information on a new collection of Communist Party USA records.

Clicking on *Thomas* takes you to almost everything you want to know about legislation: bills, their status and complete text, public laws, roll call votes, and committee reports. *Thomas*, of course, is named for Thomas Jefferson, whose donated library formed the first Library of Congress.

At the kids' site, *America's Library,* children and parents can read biographies of famous Americans; explore a time in history; find out about a particular state; investigate hobbies, recreation, and sports; view movies; hear songs; and much more.

The United States Copyright Office pages are also part of the Library of Congress site, and contain information, forms, and legislation.

The Library of Congress has created an outstanding site, a great example of the capabilities of the Web. On one hand, it is a typical library site that gives users a chance to search the catalogue, exhibits, special collections, and even view available jobs. On the other, it goes so much further in promoting the Library's services and making its collections available to all. If you are doing research on any aspect of the history or culture of America, don't hesitate to check out this site.

■ **Duke University Rare Book, Manuscript, and Special Collections Library**
http://odyssey.lib.duke.edu
Researchers in history should definitely stop at this site. The digitized collections include a wide variety of sources. Of special interest:

Emergence of Advertising in America: 1850-1920 includes more than 9,000 items (all types of print advertisements: leaflets, broadsides, cookbooks, books, pamphlets, posters, cards) are in this database, searchable by keyword or by type of illustration or special feature, such as children in illustration, sports in illustration, coupons, premiums, etc.

A related site is *Ad*Access*, which contains more than 7,000 advertisements appearing in print between 1911 and 1955. Search by keyword or browse through categories such as Beauty and Hygiene, Radio, Television, Transportation, and World War II. Illustrations and special features can also be searched. Both ad databases also include timelines.

Historic American Sheet Music presents over 16,000 pages published between 1850 and 1920. Browse by title page within dates or by subject, illustration type, advertising, or date. Historical information about the songs and a time line place them in their era in American culture.

Documents from the Women's Liberation Movement presents images of the real pages of pamphlets, fliers, and articles from 1969 to 1974. Keyword searching is available, as well as searches by subjects, such as Women of Color, Organizations and Activism, and Women's Work and Roles.

Duke Papyrus Archive features images of more than 1,300 papyri and much information about the papyri, its history, and Egypt.

Search by topics, including Women and Children, Cultural Aspects, Archives, or by language.

Check out the Duke University site for much more: presidential campaign memorabilia, an Italian pamphlet collection, women's diaries from the civil war, slave experiences, and more.

■ **The New York Public Library Digital Library Collection**
http://digital.nypl.org

The Schomburg Center for Research in Black Culture, part of the New York Public Library, collects primary source material covering the history and culture of African Americans and Africans all over the world.

African American Women Writers of the 19th Century (http://digital. nypl. org/schomburg/writers_aa19/) attests to the fact that although it was a crime to teach American slaves to read and write, many slaves did learn, and some became published authors. Interest spurred by the civil rights movement brought these authors to light. Browse by title, author, or type of writing: fiction, poetry, biography and autobiography, and essays. The full text of the work is here, as well as biographies of the authors.

Images of African Americans from the 19th Century (http://dig-ital.nypl. org/schomburg/images_aa19/) has a wide variety of photographs, engravings, and other images documenting the lives of African Americans in slavery and freedom. Search by keyword or choose from categories, such as Civil War, education, social life, politics, or individual portraits of men, women, or children. Each image is identified with a title, original caption, material type (stereograph, postcard, print, wood engraving, illustration, etc.), creator, date, source, location, and subjects (standard library subject headings).

■ **University of Pennsylvania Digital Library Programs & Projects**
http://digital.library.upenn.edu/

This site provides access to text, manuscripts, photos, maps, and audio. Read, in manuscript form, the diaries of women in the nineteenth and early twentieth centuries. Browse through a 1705 cookbook manuscript, with recipes and medicines. View corporate annual reports from a variety of companies from the 1910s to the 1960s. View the *Marian Anderson Collection of Photographs, 1898-1992,* then read about her life and listen to her sing. Search, and listen to, a sampling of more than 25,000 Yiddish and other Jewish songs in the *Freedman*

Jewish Music Archive. There is much to explore here.

■ **Cornell University Prototype Digital Library**
cdl.library.cornell.edu

This site brings the pages of books and magazines to you in digital form. Represented in the *Making of America* Collection here are primary sources in American history. Over 260 volumes and more than 100,000 articles are featured in this collection. Browse through reproductions of the actual pages of *The New England* magazine from 1886 to 1900 or *Scientific American* from 1846 to 1869, or one of many others. Investigate official records of Union and Confederate armies and navies. Browse through historical math books, or agriculture books from the early part of the twentieth century. There is much to access at this site. Check it out for even more collections.

■ **The Indiana University Digital Library Program**
http://www.dlib.indiana.edu

Peruse the *Hoagy Carmichael Collection,* which includes music, song lyrics, photos, letters, scrapbook clippings, and personal effects. Search by word or phrase. Or find the text of a novel, poem, drama, or pamphlet in *The Victorian Women Writers Project.* Search full text by keyword. Keep up with this one as other collections are in progress, including American novels, twentieth-century slides, music, and steel mill photographs.

■ **Brown University Library Digital Projects**
http://www.brown.edu/
Facilities/
University_Library/digproj/
index.html

Investigate the development of musical theater in the African American community through *AfricanAmerican Sheet Music, 1850-1920.* Read about each decade in *The Development of an AfricanAmerican Musical Theatre 1865-1910* and see actual sheet music displayed.

Or view the detailed, colorful *"Minassian Collection of Persian, Mughal, and Indian Miniature Paintings."* Much textual material is provided, besides the images.

There are a number of special exhibitions, from military characters and World War II artists to early twentieth-century Christmas illustrations and illustrations from travel books. In some cases, only part of the collection is shown, but there is usually explanatory text and a sample of the collection.

■ **University of Kansas AMDOCS: Documents for the Study of American History**
http://www.ukans.edu/carrie/docs/amdocs_index.html

Arranged by century from the fifteenth to the nineteenth, then by major events (Civil War, Reconstruction, First World War, etc.) up to the twenty-first century, each section contains charters, constitutions, reports, acts, letters, speeches, political platforms, and diaries. A great place to go for primary sources.

■ **Princeton University Library Digital Collections**
http://infoshare1.princeton.edu:2003/digital_collections/texts_images.html

A variety of texts, images, and projects await you at the Princeton Library. If you are interested in the West, check out the *Western Americana Collection, Prints and Photographs*, which includes manuscripts, Indian records, and personal papers.

Or try *Princeton University Library Papyrus Home Page*. Here you can view pieces of papyrus from many time periods, identified by author or contents, including Egyptian, Greek, Roman, and Arabic papyri, and literary, religious, and historical documents.

There are also some map sites, in particular New Jersey geological survey sheets and a sixteenth-century map of Rome to assist the study of art and architecture. This site also has links to sites at other universities that offer texts and images on line.

■ **The British Library**
http://www.bl.uk/

Click on *Digital Library* and you will find listed several projects that comprise the British Library Digital Library Programme. Here you can view facsimiles of the original *Beowulf*, Gutenberg Bible, Magna Carta, and other historical manuscripts. In addition, because Great Britain was involved in exploration and colonization all over the world, several projects from the Far East are included. One is a reproduction of the full text of *The Lion and Dragon: Britain's First Embassy to China*, a report from the 1790s.

According to information on this site, the Digital Library is a program that will continue to grow.

■ **University of North Carolina at Chapel Hill, Documenting the American South**
http://docsouth.unc.edu/dasmain.html

Southern history and literature are featured here: first-person narratives, Southern literature, slave narratives, Confederate documents, and African-American

Electronic Texts Online: Library in a Box

Many books that are no longer covered by copyright appear on websites. Although not all these sites are offered by libraries, they all provide selections from a library's most famous commodity: a book. What can you find? Classics from the ancient Greeks and Romans, nineteenth-century poetry, Tarzan novels, Sherlock Holmes stories, historical documents, folktales, sacred books from many religions, and so much more.

■ **Project Gutenberg** http://www.gutenberg.net
This is the granddaddy of all electronic text sites. It has been around for 30 years, even before the Internet's modern incarnation. Thousands of titles can be searched by author, title, subject, and language.

■ **Alex Catalogue of Electronic Texts** http://infomotions.com/alex
Featuring American and English literature and Western philosophy, this site offers searching text by keyword or browsing by author, title, or date.

■ **Bartleby.com** http://www.bartleby.com
Although this is a commercial site, access to titles is free. Search a number of reference books, anthologies, and volumes of verse, fiction, and nonfiction by author, title, or subject.

■ **Bibliomania** http://www.bibliomania.com
Search by literary type (fiction, nonfiction, poetry, reference, short story, drama), author, title, or words within the work. Designed for students, the site also includes study guides.

■ **Folklore and Mythology Electronic Texts**
http://www.pitt.edu/~dash/folktexts.html
Hundreds of tales from throughout the world appear here. The tales are translated and retold. Browse an alphabetical list of titles and authors.

■ **The Online Medieval & Classical Library** http://sunsite.berkeley.edu/OMACL
Interested in fare such as Chaucer, Icelandic sagas, or the Song of Roland? Search by keyword in text, or browse by title, author, genre, or language.

church documents and writings. More than 900 books and manuscripts are included, and some photos, covering colonial times to the beginning of the twentieth century.

- **University of California, Berkeley Digital Library Project**
http://elib.cs.berkeley.edu
This site provides California plant and animal information, maps, California environmental reports, and photos of the region.

- **The Denver Public Library Western History Photos**
http://gowest.coalliance.org
Search or browse 80,000 historic images and records from the library's Western History/ Genealogy Department and the Colorado Historical Society. They cover Native Americans and pioneers, towns and railroads, mining, art, and more. Search by author, title, subject, or keyword.

- **University of Georgia Libraries Rare Map Collection**
http://www.libs.uga.edu/ darchive/hargrett/maps/maps. html
Eight hundred maps, from the 1500s through the early 1900s, are available, most depicting Georgia and that geographic region. Search by broad subject (New World, Colonial America, American Civil War, Transportation, etc.). ■

Writer Websites: Practical & Fun

By Mark Haverstock

Along with all the serious resources available to writers through the Internet, many websites are also just plain fun. Here is a selection of sites that deliver references, writers' tips, market listings, places to chat with fellow writers, that give you those practical answers you need quickly and painlessly, and sites that are entertaining, too. We chose sites based on their interest and usefulness to writers, with an eye toward free or inexpensive access. The best way to get to know them is simply to browse and see what's available. Many have help and FAQ (frequently asked questions) sections to help you on your self-guided tours.

Be aware that websites come and go. We checked all before this book went to press, but any could fade away virtually overnight. If you can't link with the website for some reason, try typing the name into any of the search engines listed in the article before you give up. You might find the site at a new location or a site with similar content.

Don't just sit there—get clicking!

General References
■ **Bartleby**
www.bartleby.com
In addition to the *World Factbook* and the classic version of *Bartlett's Familiar Quotations,*

you'll find public-domain versions of more than a dozen widely used reference materials. You'll also find a quotation and a word for the day.

■ **Encyclopedia Britannica**
www.britannica.com

Don't reach for the encyclopedia, go here instead. Britannica gives you access to their encyclopedia entries as well as outside links for additional information.

■ **The Internet Public Library**
www.ipl.org

The collections of the Internet Public Library are divided into reference; exhibits; "especially for librarians"; magazines and serials; newspapers; and online texts. It has special collections for children and teens and many links to good sites on many subjects, including children's authors. The University of Michigan School of Information and Bell & Howell Information and Learning sponsor the site.

■ **Grammar Lady**
www.grammarlady.com

This one-woman operation raises consciousness about correct language use and reminds everyone of the ways to have fun with language. If you've got a pressing question, the Grammar Lady even has a hotline from 9:00A.M.

to 5:00P.M., Monday through Friday, with a toll-free number, 1-800-279-9708.

■ **Infomine**
infomine.ucr.edu

Infomine is especially valuable in academic searches. It includes databases, electronic journals, electronic books, bulletin boards, listservs, online library card catalogues, articles, and directories of researchers, among many other types of information.

■ **Merriam-Webster's Collegiate Dictionary**
www.m-w.com

Look up words, get help with a thesaurus, play daily word games, check out the word of the day, find language resources, and do much more on this useful and fun site.

■ **Microsoft Encarta Encyclopedia**
www.encarta.msn.com

Need some quick reference help on general topics, and without heavy reading? This is the place to go. The site also features a dictionary and atlas.

■ **Your Dictionary**
www.yourdictionary.com

Stumped by words like bloviate or diffident? Get definitions and synonyms here. If the quick lookup doesn't find them, there are links to other dictionaries and references as well, including specialty and foreign language dictionaries.

■ **United States Postal Service**
www.usps.com
Need to calculate the postage for a manuscript sent Priority Mail? Want to make sure you have the right zip code? Check this site for all you need to mail.

In Search Of . . .
■ **Amazon.com and Barnes & Noble**
www.amazon.com
www.bn.com
These online booksellers can help you locate books by author, title, and subject; get reviews; and help you purchase hard to locate books that may be out of print. Writers can do research from many directions on these sites— find research sources, do competition research, and much more.

■ **Dogpile**
www.dogpile.com/
Dogpile will fetch the information you seek from 17 popular search engines at once in all formats, including text, images, audio, and video.

■ **Google**
www.google.com
Keep it simple with just a search box, or use their expanded web directory. Google is still one of the best search engines around when it comes to accurate hits.

■ **Library of Congress Online Catalogue**
http://catalog.loc.gov
Locate books by author, title, publisher, or ISBN. The possibilities for research on this massive site are endless.

■ **Northern Light**
www.northernlight.com
This search engine provides general search capabilities as well as access to a collection of downloadable articles from periodicals. Articles generally cost less than $3, and there is a liberal refund policy if the material doesn't meet your needs.

■ **Pilot Search**
www.pilot-search.com
This arts and technology search engine will help you find everything from author information to e-zines from a growing list of more than 11,000 links.

■ **WhoWhere InfoUsa**
www.whowhere.lycos.com
www.infousa.com
Find phone numbers, addresses, and e-mail addresses,

including reverse phone number searches.

Expert Sources
■ AskMe
www.askmecorp.com

Post your question for free in any of the listed categories, from arts to travel, and wait for an answer from a professional in the field. Check the ratings to reveal the apparent reliability of your source.

■ Experts.com
www.experts.com

Do you want to find an expert in a specific field? This site matches a diverse collection of professionals with your needs.

■ Expert Source
www.businesswire.com/
expert source

ExpertSource connects writers to authoritative academic and industry sources. ExpertSource is a partnership between Business Wire and Round Table Group, Inc.

■ Journalist Express
www.journalistexpress.com

Free membership provides contacts for expert sources and a home page you can customize according to your interests. Their standard portal contains hundreds of links to specific research topics and directories.

■ Profnet
www3.profnet.com

Need a physicist for a science article or a psychologist to help explain the major fears of children? This free service connects writers to expert sources from colleges, universities, corporations, think tanks, laboratories, medical centers, nonprofit organizations, government agencies, and public relations agencies.

Internet Mailing Lists
■ Catalist
www.lsoft.com/lists/listref.html

This official site for Listserv mailing lists is a quick and free source of information and resources on a variety of topics. If you're a nonfiction writer, try searching and subscribing to lists on topics you routinely cover.

■ Publicly Accessible Mailing Lists
www.paml.net

PAML bills itself as the Internet's premier mailing list directory, frequently updating its contents. The site contains additional links to other mailing lists, as well as a question-and-answer section on mailing lists.

■ Quick Topic
www.quicktopic.com

The Internet is full of discussion boards, mailing lists, and newsgroups dedicated to specific topics. Here's a way to start your own. At Quick Topic, you simply enter a topic name and your address. You'll get an e-mail you can then forward to all the members of your group; it will contain the unique URL of an easy-to-use discussion page where folks can post messages.

Markets/Jobs
■ **Guru.com**
www.guru.com
This independent professional talent resource helps match freelancers with projects. Though not specifically for writers, it has easy-to-do custom searches for specific markets or you can create your own profile so contractors can find you.

■ **Writer's Exchange**
www.writers-exchange.com/job.htm
Check here for numerous links to jobs, news, and information about the writing profession.

■ **Writer's Weekly**
www.writersweekly.com
Freelance job listings and new paying markets are delivered to your e-mailbox every Wednesday when you sign up at this site.

Miscellaneous/Fun Stuff
■ **Backwash**
www.backwash.com

Wouldn't it be cool to have a Web-savvy pal who could clue you in to the coolest new sites? Start by picking out a personality type you're interested in: Marxist, skeptic, artsy type, etc. You'll get listings of recommended sites to check out, updated regularly.

■ **Find Tutorials**
www.findtutorials.com
Want to know how to tie basic knots, how to host a party, or how to drive a stick shift? Do a search at this site to find out these and other skills in dozens of categories.

■ **How Things Work**
rabi.phys.virginia.edu/HTW
Physics professor Louis A. Bloomfield has a mission: to answer questions about why things are the way they are in the physical universe.

■ **LiveManuals**
www.livemanuals.com
Forget how to set your inkjet printer? Program your cell phone? Find online manuals with support information for thousands of products.

■ **Marshall Brain's How Stuff Works**
www.howstuffworks.com
The hundreds of articles at this site cover categories from

Mailing Lists

You've got mail. But if you're not taking advantage of Internet mailing lists, you're missing the boat. Mailing lists can be a nonfiction writer's best friend, supplying numerous quick and free sources of information. They're especially helpful if you specialize in writing on certain topics.

Mailing lists come in two flavors, *discussion* and *announcement*. If you subscribe to a discussion list, you'll receive a message each time a member posts information. You can then read the message, reply, or generate a message of your own. One caution: When members get verbose, you can find a full mailbox. Choose wisely.

Announcement lists are most often sent from companies or news agencies—think PR release. They contain breaking news about technology, industry gossip, and other topics.

So how can these lists help you? If you need an expert, it's likely you'll find a name and phone number on an announcement list. If you need to include a real-person story in your article, you can use a discussion list to solicit contacts discreetly. You can even keep in contact with writing colleagues that share similar interests.

To join, send an e-mail to the list administrator with your e-mail address and you'll soon be added to the list. Most are automated. In some cases, like ProfNet and PR News Wire, you'll be asked to fill out a more detailed form.

When in discussions, remember to keep to the topic, focus on your point, and show consideration for others on the list. Don't forget to help others when you join mailing lists: Active participation can pay off later in valuable sources.

health to machines to the home to science. It seriously takes on questions like "which came first, the chicken or the egg?" and "how does your stomach keep from digesting itself?"

■ **SafeWeb**
www.safeweb.com
Surf the Web while maintaining online privacy through this site. Your Web address is hidden and no one will know where you've been.

Getting Connected

Maybe this is your first experience getting online, or you're an old pro looking for better service. There are now more options available, with others on the horizon. Here's the scoop on the how and where to connect from your home office today, along with some tips.

DSL/Cable. Check with your local phone or cable company. You'll love the speed, which can beat typical dial-up lines by a factor of 10 or more. But that's provided that cable and DSL are even available in your location and that they've worked out the bugs. DSL, a phone line-based service, has gotten some bad press in the last year for numerous technical glitches and poor service. In some areas, a wait of several months for a DSL installation is not uncommon and DSL has some restrictions. You need to be within three miles of a telephone switching station for it to work, which rules out many suburban and rural customers. Check with current customers in your area before taking the plunge.

Cable Internet. This is my preference. Generally, it's been more reliable and installation times can be measured in days instead of weeks or months. There's only one downside—if lots of people in your neighborhood also choose cable Internet, your connection slows somewhat, especially during peak usage times.

Satellite. You'll find it through electronics dealers such as Best Buy, Radio Shack, or Circuit City. DirecTV currently is the leading provider of satellite Internet and can provide an alternative for those who

(continued on next page)

■ **Spyonit**
www.spyonit.com
Create a personal Internet spy to notify you when a web page changes, when your stock splits, or when an airfare drops into your price range.

■ **Useless Information Home Page**
home.nycap.rr.com/useless/index.html

UIHP contains all the factoids you never needed to know, but your life would be incomplete without.

On Writing
■ **Absolute Write**
www.absolutewrite.com
A one-stop destination for freelancers with articles, market news, interviews, reviews, and a free newsletter.

Getting Connected *(continued)*

cannot get cable or DSL. These systems work one-way: You call up the Internet through your phone line and the return information is sent back via satellite. The assumption is that loading a web page takes the most time, so the satellite speeds the process. Satellite service can be pricey, but may turn out to be in the same ballpark as cable or DSL, depending on usage. The downside is you must have an unobstructed path to the south (no trees or buildings in the way), and heavy precipitation can adversely affect reception. If you already have satellite TV and you're satisfied with its performance, it's a good bet it will work fine in your location.

Dial-Up Services. Check your nearest computer stores or your phone book for local services. Dial-up services like AOL, EarthLink, MSN, and others have been the mainstay of online services for years. Though 56K connections may seem slow compared to the services listed above, they still give most Internet users reliable service and tolerable download times. Shop for the best bargains available. Often, phone companies like Sprint and AT&T will bundle your Internet and long distance services and give you discounts on both. Stay away from long-term contracts, especially ones that last more than a year. Though several retailers may offer some sweet rebates for making a three-year commitment with certain ISPs, they may not be worth it in the long run.

■ **The Institute of Children's Literature**

www.institutechildrenslit.com

This site, sponsored by the Institute of Children's Literature, provides tips for writers in the children's market, online interviews with experts, message boards, and open chat.

■ **KaZoodles**

www.datasync.com/~wordmage/kz.htm

KaZoodles is a bimonthly featuring all the e-zines, lists, books, sites and more on writing that you would like to know about but don't have time to search out. Writers are welcome to send their own writing information for inclusion.

■ **LiteraryAgent.com**

www.literaryagent.com

This database contains hundreds of agencies searchable by name, city, state, country, or area of interest. You'll also find columns on writing and forums, including one on children's literature.

■ **The Slot**

www.theslot.com

Maintained by Bill Walsh of the *Washington Post,* this site keeps a lengthy list of style points and issues, things you won't find in the *AP Stylebook.* It's a great site for the copyeditor in all of us.

■ **Suite 101**

www.suite101.com/welcome.cfm/

childrens_writing

Suite 101 contains articles on children's writing, discussion boards, and links to other sites of interest. Go back to the main site, www.suite101.com, and you'll find 1,400 general reference topics accompanied by more than 43,000 articles.

■ **Writer's BBS**

www.writersbbs.com

You'll meet fellow writers and find many resources of interest to authors, poets, and journalists here. Join other writers for writing workshops, conferences, or just to talk in our more than 50 Writers' Discussion and Critique Forums covering fiction and nonfiction. Open chat is also available.

■ **Writer to Writer**

www.writertowriter.com

Writer to Writer is a site for all writers from beginner to pro, and offers a mix of tips, articles, and advice.

■ **Writing World**

www.writing-world.com

This site picks up where the former Inkspot/Inklings website left off when it shut down. You can subscribe to their biweekly newsletter, peruse posted writing articles, or take advantage of fee-based writers' services.

Writers' Organizations

■ **Canadian Society of Children's Authors, Illustrators and Performers**

www.canscaip.org

Keep up-to-date with meetings, events, and publications.

■ **Society of Children's Book Writers and Illustrators**

www.scbwi.org

Check out regional news and events of interest to authors writing in the children's market. There's also a good collection of articles and tips excerpted from the monthly newsletter.

■ **Writer's Union**

www.nwu.org

NWU is the only labor union that represents freelance writers who work in all genres, formats, and media. You'll find current information on political issues, contracts, and other issues of interest to all writers.

On Books

- **Book Browser, the Guide for Avid Readers**

  www.bookbrowser.com

  Here's a site with reading rec-ommendations arranged by genre, features on libraries, information about authors, and more. It adds about 40 book reviews a week and gives readers many ways to find more of the kinds of books they like to read, like its If You Like . . . Try list.

- **Carol Hurst's Children's Literature Site**

  www.carolhurst.com

  While this is an educational site, with professional resources, it also posts reviews of children's sites and makes reading recom-mendations. On the curriculum areas page are lists of books to use in social studies, science, math, art, and language arts. It also has links to related sites. ■

Researching People:
The Power of Our Family Stories

By Ruth Sachs

Her life reads like the clichéd soap opera. Clara married a young lieutenant in 1875. Before their fourth anniversary, they had a son and two daughters. Clara's Julius quickly earned promotions, moving from a statewide post to a national office. A couple of months before they marked five years of marriage, Julius developed a curious disease. Clara buried him eight days later.

That life, with its multitudinous details—tragic, joyous, mundane—and countless other lives, can provide writers with ideas for plot, inspiration for characters, facts for background.

Clara mourned two husbands, four siblings, and two of her young children. The surviving son fell in battle. One of her two grandchildren died at two. But she lived to nearly 90, and sprinkled in among the deaths are glimpses of cycles of joy. Her second husband started as a clerk at a sugar factory, and retired as Treasurer. Clara's daughter married well, and great nieces and nephews went out of their way to stay in touch with a beloved aunt. The life story of Clara Ossig will never become a made-for-TV movie. It is doubtful that a children's picture book will focus on the fate of her four-year-old daughter Helene. But it can furnish a well-structured outline for a short story or for a young adult novel about life in nineteenth-century Germany, or World War I, for nonfiction pieces on life, culture, even society and politics.

The facts of Clara's story come from a source I will put back on the shelf, but not before I have derived enough narrative to keep me happily submitting for at least a couple of weeks. If I had writer's block before, it is gone now.

The source? A genealogy buried in the microfiche of a Family History Center, the genealogy centers run by the Church of Jesus Christ of Latter-Day Saints (Mormons). Free.

Unharvested Tales

If your only contact with genealogical research consists of preprinted family trees with barely enough space for birth and death dates, or the overwhelming lack of information you discover if you purchase a database like Family Treemaker, you may have difficulty believing that pure genealogy can yield very useful results. Even with graphics like charts and trees, genealogy can appear to be endless lists of 'she was born' and 'he died', with great gaps that make up the stories of our lives.

To be sure, that cycle of born-and-died has its own mesmerizing effect on the genealogist. If a researcher is lucky enough to trace ancestors back to the seventeenth and eighteenth centuries, the life cycle rhythm is inescapable.

But the cache of stories knows no bounds. For every genealogical resource available, there is a separate and distinct genre of unharvested tales, tales woven from the broad cloth of daily existence, of calico curtains and white picket fences, immigrants' misery and settlers' sweat. Of women who died too young in childbirth and men who fell in senseless wars. Of children in wagon trains, of babies dying from yellow fever, of teens who married and had families before their acne cleared up.

A War or a Life

The source that tells the tale of Clara's life provided many details to help me flesh out the setting and plot. Her first married name was Sauer, meaning *sour*, adding a layer of meaning to the plot. She moved back and forth between a large Prussian city and a small town, spending her happier days in the small town. The city, now in Poland, had a distinctly military feel.

I know the specific name of the battle in World War I that claimed the life of her son. Captain Hans Sauer was fatally wounded at the front in France at the Battle of Rossignol-

Titigny. Her daughter's "good marriage" was to a customs inspector, only a few months after World War I ended.

In fact, by the time I have finished reading the page and a half about Mrs. Clara Ossig, two or three stories have begun to take shape and write themselves on my computer screen. Do I want to focus on the historical aspects of her life and the upheaval that a world war brought to a family? I would need to research the Battle of Rossignol-Titigny if I took this approach.

Alternately, I could shine the spotlight on German history by means of Clara's life in particular. She was born the year after Germany's aborted attempt at democracy, into revolutionary fervor similar to our own Colonial period: Except that the students revolting on German campuses in 1848 were not successful, and democracy died. Her childhood was indisputably influenced by the remnants of that uprising, while her young adulthood saw Germany go to war with France, emerging not only victorious but also —for the first time in its history—united as a single nation. She lived through the rise of Communism, the first World War, and died a few months after Adolf Hitler came to power.

What a way to teach history!

The personal touch adds a dimension that takes it out of the dry and distant past and makes it come alive.

But I am also drawn to Clara on a simply human level. The aspect of a grandmother, great-grandmother telling the family story to young children who still think *old* is fascinating. The outline can be taken out of Germany, put wherever I want, and it works. Our family sagas always enthrall.

In the Beginning

Novices to genealogy need not worry about their ignorance of the subject. Most popular Internet service providers, such as America Online (AOL) and Microsoft Network, offer proprietary forums for researchers. If you are interested in tracking your own family, follow their directions to get started. The guidelines are generally well written.

If all you wish to do is tap the genealogy fountain for truth-based tales, other websites and basic sources will keep you writing for as long as you wish.

Yahoo, most often used as a search engine, is probably the simplest place to start. A portal justifiably touted for its good organization, www.yahoo.com lists its genealogy forum on its opening page. From there, information is nicely compartmentalized.

As an exercise in how such resources might be used for writing purposes, I chose the Surgener Home Page from Yahoo's index. A note from the compiler states that the Surgener family name is related to Sojourner, to which it eventually evolved. As a writer, I liked the implications of a name with hidden meaning, so I clicked on its link.

What a choice it turned out to be! Rowland *Sudgerner*, a 21-year-old from somewhere near London, swore the oath of allegiance and was transported to Virginia aboard the *Alice* on July 13, 1635. That's all we know about Rowland, but the records tell us quite a bit about John and Mary *Sojourner* of Virginia. (Remember that, historically, the same names of the same individuals may have inconsistencies of spelling.)

The researcher uncovered numerous land grants, buying and selling of property, and even John's will. He also found a legal document dated February 9, 1692: John Sojourner informed against John Collins for rustling two "beves" (beefs, or cows) from the plantation of William Baldwein.

As you can see from the records of Clara Ossig and John Sojourner, genealogical research does not purport to fill in every detail of a person's life. But in both cases, enough was written down past the born-and-died to draw up a good outline for a fiction article.

If I turn Clara's sorrow or John's propensity to rat on his neighbor into a short story, I will be making up plenty as I go along. The Ossig and Sojourner families will not call me to task if I write that Clara was a redhead and John was short, because I am not writing their family history. In fact, I will be changing some of what I know to be true to accommodate the story I am telling, as well as to stay out of hot water should I some day chance to meet the great-great-great-grandson of either family.

The Best of Sites

A genealogist who clearly understands the story-telling nature of family history writes for America Online's Genealogy Forum. You do not have to subscribe to AOL to read her work; the "Daily Genealogy Column" can be accessed on the Web. "Dear Myrtle" (www.DearMyrtle.com) combines the best of strict genealogy research—the nuts and bolts of where to find information if you are serious about your own family tree—with stories she finds along the way.

As dedicated a researcher as "Myrtle" is, she nearly overlooked an ancestress of her own named Parmilia Gist, who married into her Froman family. The Fromans, together with several other young couples, left Kentucky and moved to Missouri in the early 1800s. Myrtle writes that by 1850, Parmilia was widowed out on that frontier, left to raise several children by herself.

In one column, Myrtle mused that her serendipitous discovery made her aware "that strong-hearted women struggled to carve out a fair existence. . . . Often alone they battled the odds of the untamed prairies." Our stories tend to shine a spotlight on the men, leaving out the Parmilias and countless women like her. Their histories remain hidden in yellowed ledgers in the county clerk's office.

The Dear Myrtle column links to www.rootsweb.com, a site generally known as the Internet's oldest and largest genealogy community. For writers of historical fiction, a page of this website holds a treasure trove of first-person stories. On www.rootsweb.com/ WWII, veterans and their relatives post narratives and biographies, sometimes with photographs, of memories they would like to have preserved. Despite the WWII in the web address, the site is open to veterans of any

war, including Vietnam and the Persian Gulf.

At the site, Gaylord Merlin Yoder recounted that during the Battle of the Bulge, his squadron missed their target and dropped their payload in a patch of woods. Their mistake proved to be a winner, as they hit a German Panzer division parked there at the time.

Lewis Chinn's memory of life in a German prison camp during World War II opens a Pandora's box of questions appropriate for a Holocaust Remembrance Day discussion. He recalls the apparent theft of Red Cross parcels, one of which fed two men. He also remembers wondering if the prisoners would be gassed, "like the stories we heard about the Jews."

Keeping It Real

Since many of these men and women are still alive, their tales would not have to be fictionalized. Nonfiction writers could follow up with interviews to document history from eyewitnesses.

You will find that it is not hard to get genealogical researchers to talk. As an experiment for this article, I signed on to AOL's Family Treehouse chat. In a little under 30 minutes, I learned the following:

No one in the Family Treehouse chat thinks genealogy is dry and boring. Bob read his mother's journal and found out all the family secrets. Marie discovered that her great-uncle had been married three times. The family never knew that until she did the research and found the divorce decrees. B's great-grandparents were married December 1912 and her grandfather was born January 1913. Unnamed's mother had two children by his father before she found out he had never divorced his first wife. Queen found out that her husband's family founded Silver City, North Carolina, while her maternal grandmother's family was related to the Younger Gang. Queen added that one of her great-granduncles was a hobo that missed the train but the train didn't miss him.

These anecdotes that had chat room participants ROFL and <g>'ing from ear to ear were mixed in with serious talk about locations of documents, a Hardman who was born in Manchester and moved to Pennsylvania, and a Henry known to be a Methodist.

Yet often, knowledge of our own family bequeaths us stories so rare, so unbelievable, we almost need no other inspiration. My great-great-grandmother, the mayor's daughter, had two children out of wedlock (the first was stillborn) and married the father two months after her son was born. My great-grandmother on the other side of the family was sold to a wealthy, childless family, abused as an indentured servant. She married at 13, ran away with an alcoholic husband, bore nine children, and divorced in the 1940s.

The power of our family stories! Our synagogue hosted a "Lunch & Learn" on one small corner of genealogical research: Family Names. We have had more meaningful discussions in the past: abortion, family topics, the ethics of genetics. But more people showed up to ask questions about where they had come from than for any other topic. In some sense, our names define who we are.

If we tell these stories, our own, and those we borrow from other people, we are creating a fiction based on a reality we know. Without fail, this is a reality that invites young and old to listen, to participate, to hear with the heart. It can be found within the confines of those born/died entries commonly known as genealogy. ■

Genealogy Resources

Books

■ Ahmed, Salahuddin. *A Dictionary of Muslim Names.* New York: New York University Press, 1999.

■ Eichholz, Alice. *Ancestry's Red Book: American State, County, and Town Sources.* Salt Lake City: Ancestry, Inc., 1992.

■ *The Handybook for Genealogists. Everton Publishers,* ninth edition published in September 1999.

■ Hansen, Kevan M. *Finding Your German Ancestors.* Salt Lake City: Ancestry, Inc., 1999.

■ Helm, Matthew and April. *Genealogy Online for Dummies.* IDG Books, 1999.

■ Herber, Mark D. Ancestral Trails: *The Complete Guide to British Genealogy and Family History.* Genealogical Publication Company.

■ Horowitz, Lois. *Dozens of Cousins: Blue Genes, Horse Thieves, and Other Relative Surprises in Your Family Tree.* Berkeley, CA: Ten Speed Press, 1999.

■ Laughlin, Michael C. *The Book of Irish Families: Great and Small.* Laughlin Press, 1998.

■ McClure, Tony Mack. *Cherokee Proud.* Somerville, TN: Chu-Nan-Nee Books, 1998.

■ Nelson, Lynn. *A Genealogist's Guide to Discovering Your Italian Roots.* Cincinnati, OH: Betterway Publications, 1997.

■ Weiner, Miriam. *Jewish Roots in Ukraine and Moldova.* New York: YIVO Institute, 1999.

■ Woodtor, Dee Parmer. *Finding a Place Called Home: A Guide to African-American Genealogy and Historical Identity.* New York: Random House, 1999.

Associations

■ **African-American Genealogical Society of Northern California:** www.aagsnc.org, P. O. Box 27485, Oakland, CA 94602

■ **Czechoslovak Genealogy Society International:** www.cgsi.org P. O. Box 16225, St. Paul, Minnesota 55116. E-Mail: CGSI@aol.com

■ **Family History Centers:**
These are the indispensable research tools and they are part of every

(continued on next page)

Genealogy Resources *(continued)*

Latter-day Saints (LDS) church. To schedule an appointment to look up records on microfilm or microfiche, look under "Churches—LDS (Mormon)" in your local *Yellow Pages*. There is rarely a fee for reading, only fees for making copies. Staff is on hand to assist you with record searches.

■ **Federation of Eastern European Family History Societies:** www.feefhs.org
P. O. Box 510898, Salt Lake City, Utah 84151

■ **Hispanic Genealogy Center:** www.hispanicgenealogy.com
Murray Hill Station, P. O. Box 818, New York, NY 10156-0602

■ **International Association of Jewish Genealogical Societies:** www.jewishgen.org/ajgs, 4430 Mt. Paran Parkway NW, Atlanta, GA 30327-3747. E-Mail: HoMargol@aol.com

■ **The Irish Ancestral Research Association (TIARA):** www.tiara.ie
Dept. W, P. O. Box 619, Sudbury, MA 01776

■ **National Genealogical Society:** www.ngsgenealogy.org
4527 17th Street N., Arlington, VA 22207

■ **Palatines to America:** http://palam.org
All German Ancestry. Call 614-236-8371 for chapter nearest you

■ **Polish Genealogical Society of America:** www.pgsa.org
984 North Milwaukee Avenue, Chicago, IL 60622 E-Mail: PGSAmerica@aol.com

■ **Scottish Genealogical Society:** www.sol.co.uk/s/scotgensoc
Go to site, then e-mail for US locations (not stated on site)

■ **Historical Societies:** If all else fails, look for the nearest historical society in your area. Without fail, these include genealogical discussion and research groups.

Websites

■ **Ancestry.com:** www.ancestry.com
This site also doubles as America Online's (and Compuserve's) geneaology resource (Keyword:Genealogy). Users should be aware that the site leads the trend in charging for information, unheard of 10 years ago. Recommend using as last resort despite wealth of information.

(continued on next page)

Genealogy Resources *(continued)*

■ **Cyndi's List:** www.cyndislist.com
Over 73,000 links to useful (and trivial) genealogical websites.
■ **DearMyrtle:** www.DearMyrtle.com
One of my favorites. This woman can tell stories, plus her site is well-organized and useful.
■ **The Genealogy Home Page:** www.genhomepage.com
Sponsored by Family Tree Maker Online.
■ **Genealogy.com:** www.genealogy.com
More information, formerly associated with Family Tree Maker.
■ **It's All Relative:** www.iarelative.com
Slovak, Czech, and Eastern European Genealogy. Fun, fun site.
Includes items such as Eastern European wedding traditions.
■ **Jewish Genealogy:** www.jewishgen.org
Resources and links to good research areas.
■ **National Archives:** www.nara.gov/genealogy
A government site with many free or nearly free research tools.
■ **The National Huguenot Society:** www.huguenot.netnation.com
An example of the fact that not all genealogy is strictly ethnic or national. This is a genealogy site linked to a specific religious group.
■ **RootsWeb.com:** www.rootsweb.com
Extraordinarily useful site, and they try to keep everything free of charge.
■ **UK & Ireland Genealogy:** www.genuki.org.uk
Helpful if you want to know anything about British history and people.
■ **Yahoo:** If all of the above isn't enough, go to www.yahoo.com.
Follow the trail: Arts > Humanities > History > Genealogy and spend a couple of hours, or days, online! Then write stories.

Online Research:

In Search of Photos on the Web

By Mark Haverstock

Picture it. The right photograph can lure readers into a magazine article or make your book stand out among others on the shelf. It can illustrate how a laser works, help a reader visualize life during the Civil War, or reinforce the spine-chilling mood of a gothic novel. But finding that perfect photo can be as difficult as tracking the elusive Yeti or catching Leonard Nimoy smiling.

The Right Image

"Photo research is a bear," admits Ken Sheldon, interim Editor of *Cobblestone*, indicating the great lengths the American history magazine takes to find the right photos and illustrations. All the magazines in the Cobblestone Publishing Group use dozens of photos for each issue, and they tap four major resources to find them.

"Every issue of *Cobblestone* has a consulting editor who is an expert in the field," says Sheldon. "These people are often associated with museums and institutions. They often have resources and contacts that can point us to good photos." *Cobblestone* recently did an issue on Benedict Arnold, for example, and the Fort Ticonderoga Museum was very helpful in providing images.

A second resource is authors who submit picture ideas and sources with their manuscripts. The Cobblestone magazines also look to photo houses to fill in gaps when necessary. "But in the last few years, the Internet has become a gold mine for finding pictures," says Sheldon. "As far as starting off and getting leads, we've used the Web quite a bit." The primary advantage to using the Web, he says, is the ability to cast a broad net and search all over.

At *Guideposts for Kids* and *Guideposts for Teens,* Photo Editor Julie Brown gets a "shopping list" from her editors and art staff for each issue. "If it's something specific where stock photography will work, I'll go to stock houses like Tony Stone or FPG," says Brown. "I can call them and they'll do the research for me and send me photos, or I can go to their Internet sites, put in a keyword, and preview photos online."

If it's a news item, Brown goes to the Associated Press (AP) website. "AP lets you do a keyword search and the photo will come up," she explains. "Sometimes you have to use several different search combinations to come up with the right photo. If you put in 'Jordan,' you'll get everything from the River Jordan to Michael Jordan."

Whether it's from a stock photo house or a wire service, Brown prefers to get the pictures directly from their websites. "That's a huge advantage to us; it saves a lot of time," she says. "We've already seen the photo, we know we want it, so we can get it immediately. It's amazing how quickly it can be downloaded. Usually, I get a call within the hour to tell me it's been downloaded to our site or e-mailed to me as an attachment." If she needs higher quality images, she requests that the photos be sent on CD-ROM or Zip disk, or she may request the original photo.

Although *National Geographic* has an unmatched reputation for outstanding photo work, the kids' version, *National Geographic World,* rarely uses the in-house library. "We feel that very few photos shot for adults work equally well for children. Most of those photos don't have the kind of information or story-telling flair that appeals to kids," says Alison Eskildsen, Senior Illustrations Editor. "I look to photo stock agencies and a number of photographers, such as natural history photographers, whom we've worked with over the years. We have a good idea of what kind of pictures they have and the subjects they shoot."

If Eskildsen isn't using established photographers or stock agencies, she's surfing the Web. "We use the Web for tracking down unique sources, usually in the areas of science, history, and archaeology," says Eskildsen, "those areas where there might be experts in the field shooting pictures who would probably never market them." She cites a story on mummies: "I did a Web search. I found museums that had mummies in their collections, university professors doing historical work on mummies, dig sites, and news articles on mummies. They not only provided leads for information sources, but leads for photos as well."

The Web has really been most helpful to *National Geographic World* for science stories, hunting down high-tech information and photos. "Tech-savvy people are more likely to post the information on the Web," says Eskildsen, and "many universities are posting research on their sites."

By the Book

Editors at children's magazines usually welcome leads and suggestions for illustrations and photos, but many seek their own images and budget them in-house, relieving the writer of most responsibility. Book authors work under a different set of parameters.

Author James Cross Giblin routinely does photo research for his popular nonfiction titles. "On books like my biography of Charles Lindbergh, I've been responsible for gathering the photographs and prints to be used as illustrations, as well as obtaining the permission for their use. The publisher is responsible for reimbursing me for photographic costs, up to whatever amount is negotiated."

Whether you do your photo research on the Web or by using traditional research methods, you should begin to identify the images that will help you illustrate your book or article early in the research process.

"What I do is make a list of likely sources as I go along," says Giblin. "When I do research in other books, I might not want to use their exact photos, but I would look at their photo sources." Sometimes he finds pictures that lead him to incorporate some information in the text. Text and pictures "feed on one another," Giblin explains. He routinely makes photocopies of interesting pictures he finds, noting sources and catalogue numbers.

In the case of the Lindbergh biography, Giblin found a wealth of photos at the Minnesota Historical Society in St. Paul, not far from Lindbergh's boyhood home in Little Falls. He also found a not so obvious source in the Missouri Historical Society. Lindbergh was backed by St. Louis businessmen, hence the

Royalty-Free Images

Free pictures? Not exactly. But royalty-free images deserve a second look, especially with the growing number appearing at established stock photography houses. It's an attempt to streamline the image licensing process and keep costs down.

"With the advent of digital images, a new clip-art model is emerging in which the CD-ROM publisher pays the photographer a one-time sum, rather than a royalty each time someone licenses the picture," says Paula Berinstein, author of *Finding Images Online: Online User's Guide to Image Searching in Cyberspace*. This resembles a typical work-for-hire arrangement, unless the photographer has the foresight to negotiate an arrangement where he can sell the same photos himself, leveraging his investment.

There's a second definition. "Royalty-free may mean that no royalty is paid to the photographer if the buyer uses it in certain predefined ways," explains Berinstein. An example of this might be the hundreds, if not thousands, of photo library CD-ROMs that can be purchased for personal use, like on a website or to make personal greeting cards. If the buyer wants to use a picture for some other purpose, perhaps in a book or promotional materials, a special higher license fee applies, and the photographer receives a royalty.

According to Rohn Engh, publisher of *Photo Stock Notes*, there is a third definition for "royalty free," which generally applies to the buyer, not the photographer. The buyer doesn't have to pay extra reuse royalties like traditional or rights-managed arrangements. You pay once, and can use the image any way you want.

If you choose to use royalty-free, be sure to read the fine print and ask questions to be sure the photos you choose are cleared for publication needs. Licensing photo rights can be a complicated process, so be informed.

Check out these sources on the Web for more detailed information:

- Paula Berinstein's Online site: www.berinsteinresearch.com/fiolinks.htm
- Comstock Stock Photography: www.comstock.com
- Rohn Engh's Photosource Web Page: www.sellphotos.com

plane's name, *The Spirit of St. Louis.*

"This is where the Internet can become a big help," Giblin says. "Many historical societies, including the Minnesota and Missouri Historical Societies, have websites with indexes of their holdings, which could save you a lot of letter writing and phone calls."

Digital Images

Whether you choose photos from museums, corporations, libraries, or stock photo houses, you'll be faced with another choice: traditional prints or digital format.

Stock houses like Corbis, which acquired the extensive Bettmann Archive in 1994, are going digital to make their collection available to professionals as well as consumers on the Web. "The archive has about 70 million images—historical, news, and celebrity," says Michele Glisson, Corporate Relations Coordinator. Not all 70 million will appear on their Web catalogue. Instead, Corbis has hired photo editors to go through the images, compiling a sampling of the best to be digitized. "We're scanning the best and most demanded images," says Glisson.

Digital images bring up the issues of resolution. Resolution refers to the clarity and amount of detail present in the image, usually referred to in dots per inch (DPI). The more DPI, the better. A photo scanned at 72 DPI might be adequate for a small print or website picture, but totally unsuitable for books or magazines, which usually require 300 DPI or greater. "The higher resolution images should be sufficient for most books, newspapers, and magazines," says Glisson. "The exception would be when people are looking for a detailed portion of an image. We'll go back and re-scan the part they want, to give them the resolution they need for that detailed work."

There's also another choice to make for digital images from Corbis: permissions and licensing. "There are two models we work under," says Glisson. "The first is the traditionally licensed or rights-managed model where, for example, a magazine negotiates a price with us for an image, based on use, circulation, and their standing as a customer. The second, royalty-free, model works differently. As a user, you can go online, choose an image for a set price, $39.95 for example, and you can use that image as much as you want for commercial purposes."

The advantage to the royalty-free choice is price, and under the same arrangement you can order

Photo Research Sources

Archives and Links

- Archives of American Art (associated with Smithsonian Institute): 7th & F St. N.W., NMAA-NPG Bldg., Balcony 331 MRC 216, Washington, D.C. 20560, 202-357-2781, www.siris.si.edu
- Canadian Archival Resources on the Internet, University of Saskatchewan: www.usask.ca/archives/menu.html
- Center for the Humanities: The Miriam & Ira D. Wallach Division of Art, Prints and Photographs, Photography Collection Room 308, The New York Public Library, 5th Avenue and 42nd Street, New York, NY 10018-2788, 212-930-0837, www.nypl.org/research/chss/spe/art/photo/photo.html
- The Getty Museum: www.getty.edu/museum/main/Photographs.htm
- Library of Congress National Union Catalog of Manuscript Collections (Web interface to approximately 500,000 records for archival collections in libraries, museums, state archives, and historical societies throughout North America are searchable in this database): lcweb.loc.gov/coll/nucmc/nucmc.html
- Minnesota Historical Society: www.mnhs.org/library
- Missouri Historical Society: www.mohistory.org
- Museum of Modern Art: Collections, 11 West 53rd Street, New York, NY 10019, 212-708-9400 www.moma.org/docs/collection/index.htm
- National Archives and Records Administration search page: www.nara.gov/nara/searchnail.html
- Ready, 'Net, Go (an archival "meta index," or index of archival indexes that refers you to the major indexes, lists, and databases of archival resources): www.tulane.edu/~lmiller/ArchivesResources.html
- Repository of Primary Sources, University of Idaho. www.uidaho.com

(continued on next page)

thematic CD-ROMs, giving you a hundred or more images for $100 to $300. The traditionally licensed model, according to Glisson, offers some exclusivity: You are guaranteed you won't see the picture on the cover of a competitor's magazine next month.

But are digital photos the answer to the future of photo research—from websites or stock photo houses? Not in all cases.

Photo Research Sources *(continued)*

Books/CD-ROMS

- *Finding Images Online: Online User's Guide to Image Searching in Cyberspace.* Paula Berinstein, Information Today Inc.
  Updates to book/additional information located at:
  www.berinsteinresearch.com/updates.html
  Also check the picture resource page and directory of Web image sites: www.berinsteinresearch.com/pics.htm; www.berinstein research.com/fiolinks.htm

Directories, Databases, Web Links:

- 1 Stop Stock Quick search of 11 major stock photo suppliers: www.1stopstock.com
- A.G. Editions Photo Network: online image catalogue and the *Guilfoyle Report,* which contains industry news, annotated directories, and a current photo want list. www.ag-editions.com

"Sometimes I've had to go back to the original photo because they didn't have a high-quality digital scan for good reproduction," says Eskildsen. But savvy Web masters are beginning to respond. "They're not only posting low-resolution files, but higher quality files as well, and some will post high-resolution files if you ask."

Despite some trade-offs in selection and quality, the Web is an invaluable source for tracking down those elusive photos, and as technology improves, it may become a one-stop shopping center for image research. "The Web has dramatically changed how we do things," says Eskildsen, "by making pictures instantaneously available." ■

Index

accuracy, 1, 5, 7-8, 33, 43, 77
almanacs, 9, 48, 59, 71-72
American Library Directory, 11
anecdotes, 4, 38
annotated references, 4, 18
archive catalogues, 16
archives, 6 (sidebar), 14-17, 24, 28-29, 51-52, 60, 109
archivists, 5-7
associations, 10-11, 16, 101-102
atlases, 9, 47-48, 65, 72-74, 86
autobiographies, 13, 20-21, 80

bibliographies, 2, 8, 9-11, 18, 20-21, 24, 32, 46, 52, 55-56, 65
biographical material, 2-4, 13-14, 20-21, 25, 29, 48, 53, 58-62, 64, 67, 78, 80, 106
Books in Print, 54-55
bookstores, 4, 29, 31, 54, 57, 87

cable Internet, 91
card catalogues, 6, 9, 12, 55, 77, 79
    online, 9-19, 79, 86-87
catalogues, publishers', 8
Cataloguing-in-Publication (CIP) data, 10
CD-ROMs, 45, 47, 48, 53, 55-57, 59-61, 63, 65-66, 69, 72-75, 105, 107, 109-110
chambers of commerce, 28
Children's Books in Print, 55
children's literature, 55, 58, 66-67, 92, 94
citing Internet sources, sample entries, 46-47
college/university libraries, 11, 15-17, 28, 32, 35, 56, 77-84, 88
computers, 2, 5-6, 30, 45. *See also* electronic research, electronic/online texts, Internet resources, online research,
and Web resources/sites.
connecting to the Internet, 91-92 (sidebar)

databases, 2, 14, 17, 30-31, 50, 52-53, 55-56, 79, 86, 109-110
demographic information, 71-72
Dewey Decimal Classification (DDC) system, 11, 55
dialogue, invented, 3 (sidebar)
dial-up Internet access, 92
diaries, 2-3, 13-14, 17-20, 29, 32, 63, 80, 82
dictionaries, 3, 9, 13, 47-49, 60-63, 67-68-69, 86-87
digital images, 108, 110
directories, 11, 14-17, 23, 25, 39, 53, 58, 72, 86, 88, 110
Directory of Special Libraries and Information Centers, 11
documents, 6, 11, 17, 21, 52, 63, 76, 82-83
DSL Internet access, 91

editors, 7-8, 13, 34, 37, 39, 41, 43-44, 46, 57, 74, 104-106, 108
Education Index, 11
electronic/online texts, 83, 86
electronic research, 26, 35, 45-53, 86. *See also* Internet resources, online card catalogues/research, *and* Web resources/sites.
Encyclopedia of Associations, 10-11, 16
encyclopedias, 9-10, 13, 31, 34, 47-48, 52, 56, 62, 69, 71, 74-76, 86
experts, 3, 7-8, 34-44, 88, 90, 92, 104
    locating, 90
    online, 35-36 (sidebar), 88

family stories, 95-103. *See also* genealogical material/sources.
field guides, 70
files, 2, 5-6, 30
Forthcoming Books, 10

genealogical material/sources, 14, 17, 24, 27, 59, 65, 95-103
resources, 101-103 (sidebar)
general references, 85-86
global Internet searches, 49-50
government documents/sources, 10-11, 16-17, 21, 27, 30, 60-61, 76, 88
grammar, 53, 86
guides, 10, 14-16, 31, 56-58, 70
Guide to Children's Books in Print, 10

historical images, 108
material/sources, 2-4, 13-14, 16-17, 23-25, 27-32, 58, 60, 62-65, 71-72, 78-83, 97-99, 101-102, 105, 108
sites, 4, 13, 16, 27, 30, 33, 63
societies, 5, 14, 16, 23, 25, 32, 60, 84, 102, 106, 108-110
history,
multicultural, 20-22, 24-25, 64, 80-82, 101-103
oral, 14, 22-23
regional, 4, 14, 22-23, 26-33, 30-32 (sidebar), 65, 77, 84
women's, 16-18, 20-21, 61, 79-80

images, 6. *See also* photographic research.
celebrity, 108
digital, 107-110
historical, 108
news, 108
royalty-free, 107
stock, 105, 107-109
index cards, 2, 5

indexes, 9-11, 20-21, 23, 50, 55-56, 59, 61-62, 66, 109
Internet,
citations, samples, 46-47
connecting to, 91-92 (sidebar)
mailing lists, 35, 88, 90
resources, 7, 26-27, 34, 38-39, 46, 48-49, 53, 66, 82, 85, 86, 88, 90, 99, 104
service providers, 92, 97
interviews, 6, 8, 13, 22, 34-44, 61, 91-92
phone/online/in person, 37 (sidebar)
preparation, 40-42
invented dialogue, 3 (sidebar)

journals,
personal, 2-3, 16, 18, 20, 25
professional, 7, 34, 86

key words, 12, 48, 50, 52, 79-80, 83-84

legends, 66-69
letters,
as primary sources, 2-3, 13, 16, 18-20, 25, 63, 78, 82
query, 8
to experts, 40-41
librarians, 5-7, 11-12, 28, 50, 56, 65
libraries, 2-3, 5, 9-13, 17, 19-20, 23-25, 27-29, 32, 34, 49, 52, 55, 57-59, 62, 65-66, 71, 75, 77-84, 86, 94, 108-109
college/university, 11, 15-17, 25, 28, 32, 56, 77-84, 88, 106
online, 77-84
presidential, 17, 19
special, 6, 15. *See also* specialized sources/ collections.

Library of Congress, 16-17, 19, 24-25, 28, 30, 65, 78-79, 87, 109

Library of Congress Subject Headings, 12

licensing, 107-108

literary agents, 92

literature, 66-69

local history/research. *See* regional history/research.

magazines, 8-9, 22, 27, 30, 51-52, 65, 106, 108

manuals, instructional, 89

manuscripts, 3, 13-16, 19-20, 28-30, 78-80, 82

maps, 13, 16-17, 25, 27-28, 30, 49, 65, 71-74, 77, 80, 82

markets, 7-8, 56-58, 85, 89, 92

MLA Handbook for Writers of Research Papers, The, 46-47

multicultural material, 20-22, 24-25, 64, 80-82, 101-103

museums, 2, 7, 11, 14-15, 25, 29, 31, 35, 60, 71, 104, 108-109

mythology, 69. *See also* legends.

names, 19, 67

National Archives and Records Administrations, 17, 24-25

newsgroups/newswire services, 35, 51-52, 105

newspaper indexes, 10, 66

newspapers, 4, 10-11, 14-17, 22-24, 29, 51-52, 62, 65-66, 108

news sources, 52, 65-66

notes, 4-6, 12, 41

online,
    card catalogues, 9-19, 79, 86-87
    experts, 35-36 (sidebar), 88
    libraries, 77-84
    privacy, 90
    research, 104-110

search providers. *See* search engines.

sources, sample citations, 46-47

texts, 83

writers' workshops, 53

oral history, 14, 22-23

organization, 2, 5, 7-8, 12

outlines, 4, 8

over-researching, 12

patents, 13

periodicals, 11, 14, 17, 21-22, 24, 34, 51, 54, 56, 64, 66. *See also* journals *and* magazines.

permissions, 108

personal papers, 82. *See also* diaries, *and* letters *and* journals, personal.

photographic research, 6, 13, 16, 28-29, 33, 49, 57, 61, 72, 78, 80, 99, 104-110, (107,109-110, sidebars). *See also* images.

presidential libraries, 17, 19

primary material/sources, 2-3, 8, 13-25, 32, 60, 77, 82

privacy, online, 90

publishers' catalogues, 8

query letters, 8

quotes, 3, 8, 38, 41-44, 47-48, 68, 85-86

rare books, 16, 79-80

Reader's Guide to Periodical Literature, 10, 22, 56

records, 24-25

reference materials, 2-5, 9, 11, 34-76, 85-87
    staff, 6, 11, 28, 50. *See also* librarians.

references, annotated, 4, 18

regional history/research, 4, 14, 22-23, 26-33, (30-32 sidebar), 65, 77, 84

resolution, of digital images, 108, 110
resource material, 7-8, 11, 13-25, 53. *See also* Internet resources.
royalty-free images, 107 (sidebar), 108

samples,
    citations of Internet sources, 46-47
    searches, 10 (sidebar)
satellite Internet access, 91-92
science, 3-5, 7, 39, 69-70, 105-106
search engines, 27, 35-36, 49-50, 52-54, 85, 87, 97
searches, global Internet, 49-50
    sample, 10 (sidebar)
secondary sources. *See* biographical material, dictionaries, *and* encyclopedias.
sidebars
    "Electronic Texts Online: Library in a Box," 83
    "Experts Online," 35-36
    "Genealogy Resources," 101-103
    "Getting Connected," 91-92
    "How One Writer Keeps Track," 2
    "Internet Citations," 46-47
    "Mailing Lists," 90
    "Phone, Online, or in Person?" 37
    "Photo Research Sources," 109-110
    "Places Please," 30-32
    "Royalty-Free Images," 107
    "Sample Search: The Work Astronauts Do on the Space Shuttle," 10
    "Snares to Beware," 3
    "Take Notes or Tape-Record?" 41

"Ten Tips for a Trip to the Archives," 6
specialized sources/collections, 6, 9, 11, 14-17, 25, 79, 86
speeches, 13, 21-22, 63, 82
statistics, 11, 63-64, 71, 73, 76
Statistics Sources, 11
style, 53. *See also* grammar.
Subject Guide to Books in Print, 9-10, 15, 55
Subject Guide to Children's Books in Print, 55
subject headings, 2, 9-10, 12, 19

tape recorders, 41 (sidebar)
thesaurus, 45-48, 67, 86
translators, 49
tutorials, 89

university libraries, 11, 15-17, 25, 28, 32, 35-36, 56, 77-84, 88, 106
U.S. Government Manual, 10, 16

videos, 28-29, 49
visitors' bureaus, 28

Web resources/sites, 10, 17, 26-27, 29-32, 34-36, 46, 48-61, 64-65, 67-69, 71-72, 74-75, 77-94, 97-99, 101-110
    for writers, 56-58, 85-94
wire services, for photographs, 105
women's history/sources, 16-18, 20-21, 61, 79-80
writers' resources/organizations, 52-53, 56-58, 85-94. *See also* markets.
    workshops, online, 53

yearbooks, 59, 70-71